the

Hip
Grandma's
Handbook

Tips, Resources, and Inspiration
for the **New Breed of Grandmother**

Linda Oatman High

MARGATE CITY LIBRARY

D0969999

Published by Falls Media
565 Park Ave, Suite 11E
New York, NY 10021

First Printing, October 2007

10 9 8 7 6 5 4 3 2

©Linda Oatman High, 2007

All Rights Reserved

Printed in Canada

Design by Thomas Schirtz

ISBN-13: 978-0-9788178-8-6

Without limiting the rights under copyright reserved above, no parts of this publication may be reproduced, stored in or introduced into a retrieval system, or transmitted in any form or by any means (electronic, mechanical, photocopying, recording or otherwise), without the prior written consent of both the copyright owner and the above publisher of this book.

For my grandmothers, Minnie Haas and Emma Millard;
and for Connor and Jack,
who taught me how to be a grandmother.

14.95

14491789

Acknowledgments

Thank you to editor Justin Heimberg and to Falls Media for bringing the book to reality. Thanks to the original Hip Grandmas: Marty Crisp and Lois Szymanski.

The publisher would like to thank Tom Schirtz, Aaron Hilliard, Dave Zuckerman, and all contributing Hip Grandmas. And thanks to all the grandmas out there for everything.

Hip Contents

Hip Grandma Fashion

The Hip Grandma on the Road

The Active Hip Grandma

Hip Grandma Activities
for Three to Six Year Old Grandkids

Hip Grandma Activities
for Six to Twelve Year Old Grandkids

Hip Grandma Activities
for Teenage Kids

The Hip Grandmas Club

Hip Grandma Resources and Web Sites

Manifesto of The Hip Grandmas Club

1. Our #1 goal is to remain cool, no matter how old we get or how many grandkids we accumulate. We will be the Queens of Cool, ruling as ultra-hip matriarchs of our families.

2. We will regularly join together for support, bonding, friendship, advice, laughter, fun, and really good chocolate.

3. We vow to never, ever wear stereotypical ugly grandma clothes, drive grandma cars, or have old-lady haircuts. Our goal is to keep up with current trends, technology, music, fashion, and media.

4. Those of us who sport tattoos will not have them removed, just because we are now grandmothers. Those of us who do not yet have tattoos will consider getting one, but if we're too wimpy, we may splurge on custom-designed temporary tattoos for Hip Grandmas Club meetings.

5. We will fight like wild women for what we believe in, making the earth a better place for our grandkids.

6. We will go to concerts and rock out for as long as we are able, and we will take our grandkids to do the same.

7. We will take good care of our bodies and our spirits, so that we might be Hip Grandmas for a way long time.

8. When we are dead, our obituaries will include the fact that we were members of The Hip Grandmas Club. Our hope is that our club will last a lot longer than us.

So there. That's our manifesto. It's nothing like the Unabomber's manifesto. It's just a little bit like Martin Luther's, because we're all about peace and love and unity and happiness. We're all about remaining true to ourselves while being awesome grandmothers to our fan-freakin'-tastic grandkids.

Pledge of Allegiance to the Kid

I pledge allegiance to the kid of the united DNA of many people (including myself) and to the values for which I stand: one woman, now a grandmother, with hipness and coolness for all.

How This Club Started

I was at the beach, in Jersey, on my cell phone in a hotel room, talking to my daughter-in-law who wasn't yet exactly my daughter-in-law. She'd been my son's longtime love, his first girl, and they'd recently moved in together. I'd just had surgery, ending forever my ability to have babies, and I was mourning the loss. I was grieving big-time for those ovaries, and for the womb that'd made a good baby room. So there I was, at the beach, in Jersey, on a gorgeous September day, when the call came that would change my life.

"I had to take off work today to get a blood test," said The Girl.

"A blood test? What's wrong? Are you sick? You never get blood tests. You hate needles! What's wrong? Are you sick?"

There was a pregnant pause. (I know. I couldn't resist.)

"Just a minute." She put down the phone and walked away. "Honey?"

There was mumbled conversation, and then The Girl got back on the phone.

"Um, I'm, um, we're going to have a baby," she said.

I gulped. I sat down. I closed my eyes. "Okay," I breathed. "I have to go now and cry."

And cry I did. I cried for the loss of my own baby-making abilities; I cried for what I worried was the too-soon beginnings of my son's. I worried like crazy. I worried that they were too young. Hell, I worried that I was too young. I was only 45; my son was 21. The Girl was 22. Holy shit: I was going to be a grandmother. A freaking grandmother! I knew that there'd be a need for child care, as both parents have to work these days. Should I volunteer? How much would I—could I—volunteer? Holy crap; how could I go back to changing diapers?! How would I manage my career and a baby? How would we all do this?

Well, guess what? We've done it . . . beautifully, if I do say so myself. Connor lights up our days, Whitney Houston-esque as that corny statement may be, and my son and The Girl are doing great. They're wonderful parents, and I like to think that I'm a damn good grandmother. It's all good. The kid adores me. I adore the kid. Lesson to be learned from this: If the pregnancy is a surprise, don't worry. Be happy. This baby will be the best thing since David Cassidy; the love of your life. So go ahead and volunteer to babysit. It'll be okay. Trust me on this.

After the Con-Man was born, I was on a mission: To research and read and learn all about being a grandmother. Guess what? There wasn't much out there, and what I could find was all the diddly-squat about the old-school traditional—by which I mean BORING—stereotype of a grandmother. That traditional image is not what I'm about. So I created my own little personal library of quirky learning, and a lot of it is in this book. I include Web site resources, because the Internet is where it's at. If you don't know how to use a computer, get with it, girlfriend. (You can also check out the Web primer on page 142.) This is so not the 1970s. Call your local libraries and high schools; they probably offer classes. If not, grab a teenager and dish out some money for a once-a-week class. You'll be wicked with the mouse before you know it.

Anyway. Ever since I became a grandmother, I've been welcoming friends into what I dubbed "The Hip Grandmas Club." Now I'm welcoming you too. Let's get this party started.

Welcome to The Hip Grandmas Club

Welcome to The Hip Grandmas Club. You're a grandma (or will be one soon), but this isn't your mother's mother. No, you're way too cool for that. You're too young (the average American first-time grandmother is 47), you're too hip. There's no way that you're going to knit sweaters, not that there's anything wrong with that. You don't own a clap-on/clap-off lamp, and you've never said, "Help–I've fallen and I can't get up." If you fall, you'll get up somehow.

This is so not the stereotypical Grandma-In-A-Rocking-Chair of days past. You don't rock. Well, you do . . . but not in a rocking chair. You've been through the Summer of Love, and you've come a long way, baby. Once the embodiment of youth, you now have a new gig: grandmother. Nowadays, though, with billions of free-spirited boomers entering that role, this gig no longer means hanging up your love beads.

A grandmom's job is to sprinkle stardust into the lives of her grandchildren: to be a little bit parent, a little bit teacher, a whole lot best friend. This book is all about ways to do just that, all while making sweet and strange memories that your amazing grandkids will never forget. So you're a little bit edgy? Quirky? Just plain weird? Whatever! Go with it, chick! Do your own thing. This kid is going to rock your world.

Before the Baby is Born

chapter 1

Your Name: Make Sure It's Not Dorky

It all begins with the important task of choosing your Grandma Name. This is of great consequence—don't choose anything that you don't want to hear a zillion times. Until the day you die, you'll be a grandmother. It'll be in your obituary. I know. It's crazy.

My name is M'Mère, one of the French words for grandmother. I'm not French. I just like the way it sounds: elegant and lighthearted and chic and fun. So look at other languages when considering your name. Maybe you want to be Oma or Nai Nai or Ya-Ya. Perhaps Nonno or Grossmutter or Bube. The Phillipino Lolo and Lola are nice, and rather magical. I also like the Cherokee E dudi, despite its similarity in sound to the the bacteria that makes you sick when you eat raw hamburger meat.

Choose your name while the baby is still in utero. Make sure it's not dorky, because you're not. Savor the way your granny name rolls off your tongue. Enjoy it now, because the baby is likely to grow into a toddler who names you. Until the age of two years and three months, my grandson called me "Ma." He's got it perfectly now, and the French lilt of "M'Mere" rolls beautifully from his adorable little three-year-old mouth. I don't know how he's going to feel about it in a decade or so, but now is where it's at.

So call me M'Mere. Call me Ma. Call me Mi-Mi or Mo-Mo or Muumuu. Just don't put me in a tent dress and call me Grandma.

Grandma Names Suggestions

Baba • Granny • Nan • M'mere • Bube • Grans • Nana
Nini • Gram • Mamie • Nannie • Gramma • Mawmaw • Nanny
Mamoo • Memaw • Niny • Grammy • Oma • Grams • Memom
Ninny • Mimi • Nonie • Gran • Nona • Grandmamy • Mom Mom
Grandma • Nonna • Grandmaw • Mum

Of course, you could ignore this list and go with something totally unique: Ducky, Moogie, Gigi, GoGo, Chickie, Pinkie, GooGoo, Shimmy, Goofy. www.namenerds.com has some suggestions.

Three Steps to Getting in Good Right from the Beginning

<u>Get on the Pregnant Woman's Best Side
(Her Sexy Side) With Hot Maternity Stuff</u>

Now that you know you're going to be a grandmother, the first step to getting in good with the new little family is making the Mama feel good about herself. You remember the hormones and the tortured nights of trying to sleep on your back and the feeling fat and the anxieties, right? No matter how self-assured Demi Moore looked on the cover of Vanity Fair, you know that inside she was thinking "Does this angle make my butt look fat?" Reassure the soon-to-be-Mama with some nice booty.

Get her some sexy maternity stuff. Yes, I said sexy. Who would have thought that one day there'd be hip clothes for pregnant women? Demi Moore started it, back in 1991, and Britney Spears, Angelina Jolie, Gwyneth Paltrow, and supermodel Heidi Klum followed suit, kicking off the pregnancy-can-be-sexy trend. So get your bun-in-the-oven girl on board with some maternity clothes that rock.

> **3 Things To Never Say Upon Getting The News:**
>
> "How did that happen?"
>
> "Will you be able to afford this?"
>
> "Don't ask me to babysit."

Stylish and trendy, the wardrobe selection nowadays is so not the dreadful and matronly dregs of the 1980s. This stuff is so hot that I'd consider getting pregnant now, just to wear it. If only it weren't for that damn hysterectomy. Just Google the phrase "hip maternity clothes" and you'll get a slew of Web sites like Buddha Belly, Bellydance Maternity, Treehugger, and One Hot Mama. Brick-and-mortar stores are getting in on the act too, with well-stocked maternity sections that don't make you want to puke.

Another of the newest trends for Ms. Preggers is to get her watermelon belly decorated with henna. The pierced and tattooed chicks of today are into body art, so if this is her thing, be okay with it. Just tell her to be sure it's not the really black henna, because that has bad chemicals that can leech through the skin. Real henna—the natural light-brown stuff—is an ancient tradition and has been used on pregnant bellies the world over, with no ill effects. In fact, some believe that it blesses and protects the mama and the baby both.

Encourage her state of glowing beauty by offering to take some photos of her big belly. Take some in profile; take some closeups. Don't wince if she's wearing a thong or a belly top. (Do feel free to speak up if she's wearing a belly ring, because those things grow painfully tight when skin stretches during pregnancy.)

Take the pictures. Make her feel sexy. Replenish her wardrobe. Take her to the henna artist. You'll be golden, and she'll be glowing.

Gently Ask if They've Thought About Names

Get them a baby name book, and then keep your mouth shut and your opinions to yourself. Names from a hundred years ago are hot with young parents, and lots of babies have old man and old lady names like Henry and Gladys. Don't complain. Remember our era of hippie names, and how you briefly considered giving your kid a Zappa-esque moniker, like Moonflower Peacekarma? Okay, Moon Unit. Point made. Celebrities are naming their offspring Apple and Shiloh. These are the days of crazy names, so get with it. Do feel free to point out something the parents haven't noticed, such as the initials of a baby named Adam Steven Smith or Petra Marie Sinclair or Teresa Ingrid Thomas.

Exceptions may also be made for names that invoke nasty images of porn stars. Another case where you may want to speak up is if roll call—last name first—may affect a child's self-esteem. We who grew up in the days before self-esteem was popular remember the torment a name could cause. Every once-chubby Pat still hears the taunting echo of "Fatty Patty, two-by-four." If they're thinking of naming the baby something that will easily rhyme with an insult, point out that they're clueless parents.

The Social Security Administration reports that Biblical names took a huge upswing after 9-11, so don't threaten to build an ark if your grandkid is named Noah.

Accept the name choice, and practice saying it before the owner of the name enters the world. Don't make a nickname, because the parents really hate that.

Help Her Friends Plan a Non-Boring Baby Shower

Hey, Sunshine, you're the one with all the wisdom, so speak up to her young friends from the get-go and help to plan the shower. She's your daughter or daughter-in-law, so you should know her pretty well. Don't be a slacker. Throw her personality and passions into the shower. If she loves the color olive-green, go with the color olive-green. So what if you think it looks like cow vomit? It's her shower, not yours. Remember that.

Don't bring your own baby shower issues to the table. Don't do any of those gag-me-with-a-spoon-stupid games. Do not talk about how many hours you were in labor, and for God's sake don't mention the stitches or the sitz-baths or the three-inch rips that required surgery. Under no circumstances should you pull up your shirt or pull down your pants to show anybody your gross and disgusting c-section scars. This is not about you. Say it over and over: This is not about me.

Create good vibes by making her the shining star of the day. She's Princess Diana, before the divorce and the suicide attempts and the car accident. She's the Queen Mother. She is the mother of your grandchild, sweetie, so don't be out to lunch and mess up this event. Join forces with the other mother, your co-conspirator in grandmotherhood-to-be. If there are divorce factors, get over it and invite your ex-husband's new wife. Grow up now, Ms. Immaturity, because grandmothers have no time for that catty crap. There's no room for family feuds at this party. Get your head together, keep it kosher, and lay low. You are not the star here.

You had your baby. You had your wedding. One day you'll be the star of your own funeral. Don't make it too soon by screwing up the baby shower.

Hip Tip

This book recommends a lot of websites and on-line shopping destinations. In fact, you can even read this book in front of a computer, in case you want to look up a website right away. If you are technologically challenged, no problem—turn to page 142, where you will find "A Grandmother's Non-Complicated Guide to the Worldwide Web."

Some Neato Baby Shower Stuff

1. **Handmade soap,** personalized with your choice of words and pictures, is an impressive party favor and much more useful than those moronic little plastic diaper pins that serve no apparent purpose. Search the Web for "personalized soap" and you'll find a number of vendors.

2. Believe it or not, some people are now holding **baby showers online.** Yes, you too can host a virtual baby shower, where even those living far away from the expectant couple can spend money and send gifts! Too bad that birthing can't be done with the click of a mouse. (**www.webbabyshower.com**)

3. If you insist on playing some games, non-dorky ones may be found at **www.babyshower101.com.** Don't forget to invite men to the shower. Some will actually come, and others (better still) will just send money.

The Adopted Baby: Don't Worry; You'll Love Her Just as Much

Maybe there's no pregnant woman to pamper with hip maternity wardrobes. If the parents are adopting, you're still a grandmother-in-waiting. Even if she doesn't come from your bloodline, the adopted grandbaby will reign as queen of your heart. You'll love her just as much as the ones related by blood, even if she doesn't have your weird stick-out ears. She's part of your oddball family now, but don't forget to honor her heritage. Get some books, artwork, and mementos of the culture and country into which she was born. If she was born in the U.S. of A., forget that stuff and just love her.

1. Awesome flag blankets may be found at **www.yammi-boutique.com**. The boutique division of their company also makes pageant wear, but please don't get the kid into that frightening field. Little beauty queens with false teeth, lipstick, Tammy Faye mascara, and teased hair are scary.

2. The Dream Kidz Society is a grassroots movement that provides support and mentoring for adoptive families. Their gift shop offers memory books and other dreamy gifts. You can find them at **www.thedreamkidz.com**.

3. Mandy's Moon offers Vietnamese silk paintings, Asian dolls, My Roots clothing, and other multicultural goodies. (**www.mandysmoon.com**)

3 Things Not to Say Upon Meeting the Adopted Baby:

"She looks like . . . Like . . . YOU! Isn't that serendipity?"

"Do you think he'll ever want to meet his real parents?"

"I just wish that there was a baby with my eyes.
Well, maybe some day."

Earn Points By Giving the Soon-to-Be Parents a Babymoon

The trendiest new trend among young expectants is to go on a "babymoon." You know, like a honeymoon except the woman is fatter, and there's not as much action. This is their last hurrah before the bundle of joy arrives, so think about chipping in on a weekend in a tranquil place. (And no; you shouldn't ask to go along, too. Yes, a babymoon is for three people, but that means Mama, Papa, and the Unborn One. Not you. Stay out of it. It's good to start practicing now.)

The term "babymoon" can also mean Mama, Papa, and the Just Born One. Parents nowadays seem to be much more free about lugging brand-new babies on vacation. Plus they have more money than we did. Good for them. If they have more money than you do now, don't worry about chipping in. Just suggest the idea, and you'll be golden. Here's a great Internet resource for babymoon ideas: **www.babymoonfinder.com**. It's got gobs of ideas and suggestions for those bursting with questions like "Where's the nearest hospital?" and "Do they offer pre-natal massage?" and "Will the bathrobes fit?" Ashley King, who runs the site, has researched at least fifty destinations. I don't have half a hundred suggestions, but here are three great places where I've stayed (albeit not pregnant, and not with a baby, but whatever):

1. **Congress Hall in Cape May, New Jersey.** John Philip Sousa stayed there. It's on the beachfront, it's old, and it's comfortable. The linens are wonderful, and the Big Tummied One will sleep ever-so-soundly. There's the famed Cape May Day Spa in town, so Ms. Preggers can get a facial and a massage and all that good pampering stuff. I stayed in The Blue Room, and I could see the ocean from every window, even while sitting on the toilet. If you think that's too much information, get over it. Somebody's going to be giving birth, and modesty goes right out the window. (**www.congresshall.com**)

② **Christopher Place in Newport, Tennessee.** Nestled in the Smoky Mountains near Gatlinburg, this is the ultimate in B&B luxury. There's a winding spiral staircase, and a "Gone With The Wind" vibe. Voted one of the most romantic inns in the U.S., Christopher Place is a haven for lovers. And she won't even have to worry about getting pregnant. (**www.christopherplace.com**)

③ **The Sherry Netherland in Manhattan.** With views of Central Park and huge rooms, the mother and father-to-be will unwind in Big Apple Heaven. White-gloved attendants push the elevator buttons for guests, and employees are at your every beck and call. In a little while, this couple will be under the Little Boss's command, so this will be a real treat. Central Park carriage rides beckon from across the street, and the hotel is a hop and a skip from FAO Schwartz. Not a bad idea for the parents to visit FAO without a kid in tow, so they get to have the uninterrupted, no-whining kind of fun. (**www.sherrynetherland.com**)

Hip Tip

Save the new baby's cord blood. This tip alone is worth the price of the book. Wish I'd have known about it when my grandbaby was born. There's precious stem cell stuff in that placenta and umbilical cord, and it usually ends up in the trash. Now, however, there's a way of banking it, and it could save the life of somebody in your family. ***www.cordblood.com.***

Hello in There . . .

You know those ultrasound photographs that look like a space creature is floating inside the pregnant woman, but she and her hubby think it's the cutest thing they ever saw in their entire lives? They stare and stare at those pictures, and carry them in their wallets. Actually, when I was a grandmother-in-waiting, I gazed at my grandbaby's ultrasound, too. It looked like an alien smoking a Virginia Slims cigarette, but I loved it anyway. I didn't know what "it" was, so I named it Connor-Bella, a combination of the boy name (Connor) and the girl name (Isabella). My son, the baby's father, said that his baby would have a complex. He doesn't. Here are some ideas for cool, different things you can do with those ultrasound pics.

1. I discovered a way-cool thing way-too-late, but I think I'll splurge for one anyway. Ultrasound paintings by artist Heather Tapia turn those alien photos into the most beautiful works of art. Overlaid with shimmery opaque and metallic oil sticks, the sonograms are permanently glazed with a shiny high-gloss varnish. (**www.ultrasoundpaintings.com**)

2. This is uber-cool: Storksview Ultrasound offers the most amazing 3D ultrasounds of unborn babies, combining cutting-edge technology with a comfy family viewing environment. Imagine sitting in front of a big-screen TV, and watching a video of your grandchild-to-be, turning and rolling and yawning. Located in Tampa, Florida, this might just be worth the price of a flight. Go to their Web site and click to view an actual video: **www.storksviewultrasound.com**. It'll blow your mind, in a very good way, if you don't get squeamish at the sight of umbilical cord.

3. Display the grandbaby's ultrasound photo in a cutesy keepsake frame from **www.pregnancystore.com**. If your co-workers ask about the tiny extraterrestrial on your desk, just mumble something about being abducted by an alien. You're not lying; soon enough it will be true.

House Play

I am a realtor and have taken my three year old granddaughter to see many homes, inspections, realtor "Tuesday tours," etc. She is so used to it that she will walk around opening closets and say things like "Wow, great closet space!" or "This kitchen needs to be redone."

If I am on a street where we have seen a house in the past, she might say, "Oh, there's that yucky house." She loves to go on Tuesday tours to get lunch and now has expectations of really good catered food when she goes. She also can be heard talking on her toy cell phone saying, "I would like to show your house today." She thinks I have a fun job.

I have a lot of real estate signs in my garage. Yesterday she was over and riding her play car around my back driveway and she wanted me to put up the signs around the yard so she could drive around and "show" houses to her "client".

—Linda Saveland
Hip Grandma
Rockville, Maryland

3 Things Not to Say Upon Seeing the Ultrasound:

"What's that thing? That thing right . . . there?"

"I saw this show on the Discovery Channel where the ultrasound looked a little funny, and they thought it was just a cleft lip, but it turned oout to be so much worse . . ."

"It looks a little small. Are you eating enough?"

Brand New Hip Grandma

chapter 2

How to Hint That She Should Breastfeed Without Being Too Annoying

Okay, so in 1983 I belonged to a group called the Nursing Mothers. I breastfed my first son until he was almost three, and to this day I can still imagine my milk letting down at the sight of a nursing baby. I was the definitive poster child Earth Mother, and I really, really wanted my daughter-in-law to nurse. She didn't. I hinted, though, and you can too. Say "Breast Is Best" without opening your mouth. Just get out your credit card and order these:

1. A breastfeeding support kit from **www.hipandlittle.com.** The kit includes nipple butter, booby tubes, and milkmaid tea. Enter "breastfeeding support kit" in the search field on the site.

2. An over-the-shoulder baby holder from **www.parentsafely.com.** Even if she doesn't nurse, this'll come in handy for toting the tot. And when the kid's too big, maybe she'll go all Paris Hilton on you and put a little frou-frou dog in there.

3. An inexpensive bracelet that keeps track of which breast is next. Find them at **www.milkbands.com.** If she doesn't nurse, she can wear it just for fun, hopefully giving her a guilty pang each time she glances at it.

3 Reasons Why I Nursed
(But You Don't Need to Say These, Because it Won't Make Any Difference Anyway):

It saves money.

It's healthier.

It's easier.

If the Baby is Bottle-Fed
No Matter What You Say, Do, or Buy

It's time to suck it up and shut up, because you're not going to change anybody's mind. The kid will be fine. Trust me on this. Here are some cool products for the bottle-fed baby:

1. A cow baby bottle: The bottle is spotted black and white, and the nipple is an udder. It's so kitschy, weird, and udderly ridiculous that the parents will look at you funny. (**www.sparkability.net**) Click on the mealtime bar at the bottom of the Sparkability page for the cow baby bottle.

2. Earth's Best Organic Baby Formula: If they're going to put something in a bottle, this stuff is extra-good. You can find good baby formulas all over the web. Don't worry about the more commercial baby formulas either. It's all good. There's a lot of research behind all of that stuff.

3. Yes, you carried your bottles everywhere you went without a bag, but this is so not about you. Take a look at your droopy boobs, and then run to your computer to get the bottle feeding parents a sophisticated designer diaper bag in which to carry those bottles and formula. (**www.diaperbagboutique.com**)

Hip, Hip Hooray!
You're hip, so of course the kid is going to be born hip. Get that little hipster some hip clothes at **www.bornhip.com.**

Three Tips for Adjusting to Life in the Hood

1 Get out your tightrope walker costume, because grandmotherhood is a balancing act. Life in the hood can be dangerous. The new parents' emotions are raw, so don't throw salt on them by overstepping your boundaries. Give them some alone time. Give them some help. Let them think it was their idea.

If your schedule allows, and if you want to do it, volunteer to come to their house to help out. Answer the phone; do the laundry; wash the dishes. It won't feel like you're doing chores, because there's that beautiful new baby within your reach. I went to support my daughter-in-law as her c-section stitches were taken out, because not only did I get to hold her hand, I got to hold the baby. Good payoff, despite the squeam factor.

2 Try not to talk, think, breathe, eat, and sleep the baby. Keep going to work. Do your laundry. It sucks to be in the same room with a grandmother who's worn the same clothing for seven days straight. When my grandson was a week old, he spit up on me. I was proud of it. I smelled like a baby... a stinky one. I wore the shirt all day, because I kind of liked the stain (hey, it was heart-shaped, okay?!) My youngest son informed me that I smelled really, really bad, and that I needed to change my shirt. I did.

3 Don't call their house constantly, because you're going to keep waking the baby and that'll make the parents cranky. Emails and IM's are okay, just in case you really, really need to check up. Don't make the parents sound incompetent, though, as with an email reading something like "You're feeding the baby often enough, right?"

Get This for the Mommy

Whether she's your daughter or your daughter-in-law, the new little apple of your eye does have a mother. You've got to pretend that you didn't forget her; she's the one who gave birth after all. Just because you're in menopause doesn't mean that you can't remember the labor and the pain and the leaking breasts. Get the mommy some stuff that's all about her, but also kind of about the baby too.

1. Memory Maker Bracelet. It's a bracelet with little picture frames she can fill up with photos of the Baby Divine. While you're at it, get one for yourself too. (**www.memorymakerbracelet.com**)

2. Key to My Heart. A cool keychain sparkling with Swarovski crystals and the baby's birthstone and name. She'll never misplace her car keys again. (**www.keytomyheart.net**)

3. A Crystal T-shirt. While you're on the crystal kick, get the new mama a custom-designed rhinestone T-shirt glittering with the quintessential Swarovski. Crystals are a girl's (and grandma's) best friend. (**www.justjen.com**)

3 Things Not to Say to the New Mommy:

"Have you lost all the pregnancy weight?"

"Doesn't his diaper need to be changed?"

"Isn't it time that she's sleeping through the night?"

Get This for the Daddy

Gifts aren't just for Mama anymore. Make sure that your son or son-in-law is happy too. (Don't forget that he might be just a little bit testy, because, um, you know, it's been a while since he had sex.) New fathers sometimes feel overlooked and yes, even jealous of the baby. Deep inside he's still a little boy, and he needs some nurturing. He also needs some networking. A bunch of new dads in California were on to a good thing in 1990 when they started the Boot Camp for New Dads. Using a manly-man approach, these guys go all over the place, educating their fellow men on how to bond, bathe, change, and play. They even work with the Army and the Navy and the Air Force. Can't get much more manly than that. Check it out at **www.bcnd.org**.

Sneak in some alone time with your son or son-in-law, and try to get him to talk about his feelings. (Yeah, right. I know. It ain't gonna happen. But at least you tried.) Praise his parenting. Get him some stuff, and make sure some of it's not about the baby, because we all know that the male ego needs reassurance that it's really all about him.

Get the new father a Dadgear backpack or messenger bag: If he doesn't want to use it for diapers and bottles, it'll come in handy for other stuff, like Playboy magazines. Go to **www.showeryourbaby.com** and click on "Daddy Gifts."

3 Things You Should Not Say to the New Father:

"Don't drop . . . aieee . . . don't drop the baby!"

"Be careful."

"This baby is fragile. Like an egg. If you drop it, it breaks."

Religious Gifts

Even if you're not into church, your grandbaby might be.
Religion is coming back into style with the younger generation,
probably due to the sucky state of our world nowadays. Sometimes
new parents get religious after the birth of a baby. Witnessing a
miracle will do that to you.

In search of the sacred, many parents are into church and higher
powers. Faith and hope aren't bad things, so support their desire
to connect with the holy. If you're religious too, but they choose
a different religion from you, don't kvetch. Love is love and faith
is faith, and they are their own people. They are grownups. They
can believe in whatever they want to believe. Chant this over and
over, like a mantra, until you believe it. Support their choice to be
religious with these godly gifts:

1. The Baptism Blanket: A personalized, super-soft silky
   blankie heirloom to commemorate a baptism, christening,
   or dedication. (**www.thebaptismblankie.com**)

2. An angel to watch over him: Who can argue with a
   guardian angel to watch over your precious grandbaby
   and keep him safe? Even if it's a bunch of BS, the prices are
   right, so you can't go wrong. Click on Faith and Religion
   on **www.sucasagifts.com**.

3. A Jesus-Loves-Me Basket: Save your soul with this collection
   of cool stuff for the Christian kid. (**www.basketsoffaith.com**)

Hippie Gifts

If you're a baby boomer, you're may well be an ex-hippie or still a pseudo-hippie. Does the soundtrack of your life sound like a Grateful Dead record? Even if your offspring became Young Republicans, encourage the grandkid with a mild G-rated version of hippie-hood. Don't be surprised if your grandchild's parents become the polar opposites of you. I raised my children to be free about nudity, but my son and his wife don't believe (never did; never will) in the values of bathing with your baby. I nursed; she didn't. (Sniff. Pout. Okay, get over it and move on.) Prove how Earth-grandmotherish you are with these tree-hugging gifts for the brand-new family:

1. Baby clothes that Jerry Garcia would be proud of from **www.soul-flower.com**. Tie-dye—right on!

2. Environmentally-conscious cloth diapers with a hippie twist can be found all over the web. Just google "hemp diapers" and you will be surprised how much comes up.

3. Door beads for the hippie nursery: Make sure to croon "Sweet Magnolia" and other Dead songs in that far-out nursery. They make groovy lullabies, and the kid might just dream of dancing bears. (**www.didyousay.com**)

Keep the Peace

Best Case Scenario for Grandmotherhood is that the grandmothers be friends, not competitors. Don't keep score of money or time or teddy bears or toys.

3 Things Never to Say to the Co-Grandma:

"So how many times have you had him overnight?"

"Does she cry when you hold her?"

"How much did you spend?"

Now that You've Sucked Up to the Parents

Now that you've sucked up to the parents, it's time to start winning the grandbaby's heart. Ten things that you should have done by the time the Grandest One reaches the age of one:

1. Give the kid his first taste of ice cream, preferably when the parents aren't around.

2. Stand on your porch, and as the parents pull into the driveway with the Revered One, jump up and down and act like a monkey (or a hyena or a dog or a bird).

3. Make funny faces and strange noises. Make strange faces and funny noises.

4. Play peek-a-boo again and again and again. It never gets old, and neither do you.

5. Crawl on the floor. Crawl some more. Crawl even when you're bored.

6. Hold the baby to the ceiling and pretend that he's Spiderman.

7. Fly the baby through the air and call her SuperBaby.

8. Bounce her on your leg and call yourself a Horsie. Neigh. Whinny. Eat apples and carrots, and let the baby taste them too.

9. Sing along with dorky baby songs. Change the words of "Elmo's World" to (baby's name) World."

10. Pretend to be a baby. Drink from his bottle. Cry. Laugh. Whine. Sleep. Get the baby to sleep too. Take a nap together, because all this baby-pleasing is tiring and really kind of boring at times. Do it anyway. You're just setting the stage for the fun stuff to come.

It's So Totally Tea Time

Every little girl—and boy—should have a tea party by the age of three. A Victorian tradition that teaches manners and grace, tea parties are a time for relaxation and talking with a British accent. Who can argue with that? Put on your fancy-lady hat, act elegant, make some eensy-weensy finger sandwiches, and have a grand time with your well-behaved Victorian children.

1. Get a superb tea party set that'll be cherished for years and be handed down as an heirloom long after you're gone. (Dismal thought, huh? Don't worry: The tea party will cheer you up!) (**www.bluemoontea.com**)

2. Make healthy vanilla-milk tea with the tiny tea-drinker. Here's the recipe:

    1 cup milk

    2 tsp. vanilla extract

    4 tsp. green tea (or 4 green tea bags)

    1 quart boiling water

    Pour the milk into a saucepan, add the vanilla, and bring to a simmer, stirring often. Remove the pan from the heat and let it stand until the milk is cool. Place the tea leaves in the teapot and add the boiling water. Cover with a towel and steep 5 minutes. Pour about 1/4 cup of the cooled milk into the teacups. Stir and strain the tea into the cups. Makes 4 to 5 servings.

3. If you have a granddaughter, get her a tea party tiara from **www.rhinestone.com**. Don't get one for your grandson, although it'd probably look cute. It's pathetic enough that you made him sit through a sissy tea party. Get him a newsboy cap from **www.dapperlads.com** instead.

The Seven Sacred Rules for Grandmas

Oy vey. The Rules keep changing, but here's the newest wisdom from the Doctors Who Advise New Parents, who in turn sometimes morph into New Nazi Parents with their inflexible commands to quaking grandmothers.

1. Babies should sleep on their backs, not on their tummies. Sure, it looks cute when their little butts stick up in the air like that, but the newest research on SIDS (sudden infant death syndrome) connects it to belly-sleeping. So put the kid on his back for bed.

2. No honey or peanut butter until after the age of two. I don't know the reasoning behind this, but at the very least it's really sticky on the roof of the mouth, and you don't want the kid's lips to be glued shut.

3. No cow's milk until after the first birthday. That stuff is for baby cows, not for your grandbaby. After all, calves don't drink human breast milk, do they? Point made.

4. Check with the parents about pacifiers. Some want them, some don't. If the parents say no, and you're babysitting, keep a secret binky hidden in the cupboard. They'll be none the wiser, as long as you give the kid's skin enough time to lose the imprint around the lips. Take the pacifier out twenty minutes before the parents' estimated time of arrival, in order to be perfectly safe.

5. Wash your hands before touching the baby. One of my friends, a super cool grandma, flew south to see her brand-new grandson. She and her husband ran up the tarmac and into the airport, so excited to see the New One. However, upon reaching the waiting area and grabbing for the infant, my friend was informed by the Daughter-In-Law that she had to wash her hands. Now. Before she touched the baby. Geez. So wash your hands. Carry those little bottles of soapless

antibacterial, so you don't have to make a long trek to the ladies' room.

6. No juice before age one, because the sugar might cause diabetes. Grandbabies on insulin are not cute if you're the one who caused it.

7. The rule of all rules: No matter what the parents or experts say, do what you think is best. After all, you did keep a baby alive at one time, or you wouldn't be a Hip Grandma today.

Some Advice from the Boomers to the Bluetooth Generation

Much as you try to keep your mouth shut, there are some things that the baby's parents have to hear from you. Tell them to keep that stupid Bluetooth headset off their ears when they're at the zoo or in the park with the kid. Forbid them to yak on the cell phone while driving with the precious cargo that's your Divine One. And this happy hour playdate stuff? Tell them we got through the boo-boo kissing and butt-wiping just fine without five glasses of wine at playdate. Don't go all Dr. Spock on them. Just casually give them your two cents worth, and then write on their refrigerator with magnetic alphabet letters: VODKA AND BREAST MILK DO NOT MIX.

Ignore All that Stuff about How Kids Shouldn't Watch TV until They're Over Two

There's been some bad press recently about how it'll make kids really stupid if they watch television or DVDs before the age of two. I say ignore that stuff. It's bogus. The television screen is not the devil's playground. Nothing says "Grandma's house" like snuggling on the sofa and enjoying a great DVD. Here are some educational ones that won't make your little prodigy dumb.

"Baby Chatterbox"

"Baby Babble"

"Brainy Baby Laugh & Learn"

"Sesame Street: Do The Alphabet"

"Sesame Beginnings: Beginning Together"

"All About John Deere For Kids"

"On Site With Thomas and Other Adventures"

"Motorized Madness"

"Kiddie Village: Let's Play Music"

"Busy Little Engine"

"Galloping Minds"

Because the Talking Toilet Paper Says So

And for those enjoyable toilet-training times, here are the three best DVDs in Pottyland. Expect to walk around humming "pee pee goes there; poo poo goes there" for days after watching the first one.

"Once Upon a Potty"

"Potty Power"

"No More Diapers"

Here are two other cool things for their porcelain paradise:

1. Don't forget to have a potty chair for the little king at your castle. Throw in some silly novelty toilet paper. You can get rolls with duckies and lucky charms and Valentine hearts from **www.justtoiletpaper.com**.

2. Potty training dolls Emma and Paul drink from bottles, then wet in their own potties when you squeeze their bellies. Vanilla scented, these well-made French dolls please the parents (and grands) as much as they do the kids. An added bonus for little boys is that Paul is anatomically correct. If you're still harboring that old-school notion that little boys shouldn't play with dolls, get over it already, old woman. (**www.corolle.com**)

The Ten *Grand* Commandments

Now that you know the seven rules, it's time to memorize the ten commandments. Repeat these over and over, inscribe them in stone if need be, and practice them so that you are not sent to Grandma Hell, burned for eternity by the wrath of The Parents.

1. Thou shalt put no other kids before thine grandkid.

2. Thou shalt always have an image of thine grandbaby in thine wallet.

3. Thou shalt not make a nickname of the given name chosen by the parents.

4. Remember thine grandbaby's birthday, and keep it holy.

5. Honor the father and mother of the grandbaby.

6. Thou shalt not kill the expectations, dreams, or beliefs of the parents or the baby.

7. Thou shalt not make paltry comments about the cleanliness of their home.

8. Thou shalt not steal the parents' sovereign power.

9. Thou shalt not bear false witness against their labor in raising their baby.

10. Thou shalt not covet their relationship with their baby.

Repeat it over and over:

Their baby. Their baby. Their baby. Their baby . . .

Amen.

Loving Matthew

His face is snuggled against my shoulder. The feeling is indescribable. I feel his warmth and lower my head to kiss his baby-fine hair. The scent of peach shampoo clings to him and I breathe it in. I bury my face to kiss him. I'd forgotten how good it is.

That trust, that total dependency feels good but I don't know why. I don't question it. I just love him. I hadn't expected to be a grandmother so quickly. I hadn't imagined how it would feel to hold this baby boy and love him as much as I loved my own two girls.

His eyes flutter open, and just like always, he smiles immediately. This grandson of mine always wakes up happy, thrilled to be awake and with us. No matter how I feel before I see him, my heart warms to total sunshine when he smiles my way.

I am honored to be the one taking care of him while his mommy works. I hadn't planned this at all. I left my job a short time ago to write full-time. Now instead I am babysitting full-time with no regrets. There isn't a moment that I want to be somewhere else. There are many, many moments I am overcome with joy to be the one holding his hand, feeding him lunch, rolling trucks across the floor, matching shapes in a shape-sorter, reading books to him, laughing with him.

There is no higher form of amusement than watching Matthew play, listening to his chatter and only recognizing an occasional word. His imagination amazes me.

One day he finds an old bingo dauber in a drawer. He carries it across the room, stopping beside the coffee table. Carefully, he lifts it and dabs the top end in one hand and then the other. He sits it down on the table and rubs his hands together carefully, just as he has watched his mommy do when she is putting lotion on.

"Matthew!" I call and he jumps because he didn't know I was watching. "Can I have some lotion?" His face lights up and he toddles across the floor to dab my hands with the closed top bottle. I understood what he was doing, and he is thrilled with me.

At his first birthday his parents give him a truck that he can sit on, push a button on the handle and make it go. It doesn't take him long to learn how to make it move. He rides it often, but doesn't know how steer, so he runs into walls and furniture, then spins wheels until someone turns him around to go in another direction. He's fun to watch.

One day he rides the truck across the floor and into the front door. He looks at me, wheels spinning, and then gets off. He stares at his truck, analyzing the situation. I watch in amazement as he gets back on facing backwards. He reaches back and pushes the button. His face registers disappointment when the wheels spin against the front door. His logic amazes me. He couldn't turn the truck around, so he turned himself around! Why do such little things make me so proud of my grandson?

He's only fourteen months old when I realize that Matthew has an internal clock. Just before 4 p.m. each day he toddles to the window and gazes out. When his daddy's work truck pulls into the driveway, I hear Matthew say, "Da da!" He says it quietly, almost a whisper, like a discovery rolling off his tongue. His daddy gets out of his work truck and the "Da da, Da da," gets louder. By the time his father is at the front door Matthew is giggling out loud, an infectious sound that floats on the air and makes me laugh along.

"Oh-is!" he calls when I come in the front door in the morning. All those months of telling him to give Grammy a hug mean nothing to him. He has heard others call me Lois so that's what he calls me. I crack up laughing and swing him high in the air. I am his "Oh-is" and I am darned proud of it!

There's nothing better than being a grandmother. I love it. I live for it. I wouldn't change a thing about it. I'm honored to be a member of The Hip Grandmas Club and I plan to stay a member for life!

—*Lois Szymanski*
Hip Grandma
Westminster, MD

The Hip Grandma's Home

chapter 3

Turning Your House
into a Granny Place

If you live within three hours of the grandchild, you've got to outfit your house, because that baby will be coming over the river and through the woods. To grandmother's house they'll come, whether it be by minivan or BMW, and you want to be ready. You also want to prove to the baby's parents that you're well-equipped to baby-sit for an evening or a weekend. Here are three items guaranteed to make you seem quite competent enough, thank you very much:

1. A Pack-and-Play. This is essential, the first thing you should buy, and it'll work for a long time. You can get them wherever fine Pack-and-Plays are sold. If you insist on using an old crib, be sure that there's at least 2 and 3/8 inches between bars.

2. A baby hammock: Because babies can never get too much sleep. Made down under in Australia, these hammocks are guaranteed to sooth, especially babies with colic, preemies, and ill infants. Impress the baby's parents with the fact that you have found something they have not. Pretend that it's because you're a worldly traveler, and keep it on the down low that you really just discovered it on the Internet: **www.babyhammocks.com**.

3. A high chair: Because eventually the kid will eat. Get one that looks cool in your kitchen, like maybe the Made in Italy one that grows with the child. When you're not babysitting, the high chair is a good place to pile the bills and junk mail. (**www.bonnybabies.com**)

Stop Bitchin' in the Kitchen

So we came of age in the I-Am-Woman-Hear-Me-Roar-That-I-Don't-Cook era. We bring home the bacon, but we want somebody else to fry it up in the pan. Women's rights did us in. We burned our bras and our boobs got saggy. We threw out our pots and pans, and everybody went hungry. The women's movement took us out of the kitchen, and into the workplace. McDonald's and Burger King had a heyday, and we all got fat. Now it's time to get back to the basics: food, food, and more food. Cooking is cool, now that Rachael Ray has hit the scene. We who grew up with Julia Child and the Galloping Gourmet ran from the kitchen in droves, thinking it non-hip to flip the omelette. Come on back, girlfriend. You won't turn into a Stepford Wife if you spend some time over the stove, whipping up something delicious with the grandkid. You can find lots of advice on cooking for kids plus complete cooking kits on the Internet; **www.craftycookingkits.com** is a good place to visit for both. I dig the Ice-Your-Own-Animal-Cookies kit, and also the Funny Face Rice Krispies Treat kit.

Some more ideas:

1. Every grandmother needs a good coffeemaker. If you're a babysitting grandma, the caffeine will get you through the day. A really cool java-maker is the Capresso. Grind those beans. Brew that brew. (**www.capresso.com**)

2. Swiss company Kuhn Rikon makes the coolest red Hotpan Cook and Serve set. It seals in vitamins, uses less oil and fat, and it's easy and stylish and looks good in your kitchen. It's hot: sssssssss. I also love their epicurean garlic press; it's an exquisite and efficient way to get garlic into your dishes. Fresh garlic is ever so good for you, and it keeps the vampires away. Just don't pick up the kid right after pressing the garlic. Wash your hands first with the new Zilo-Soap. It removes odors of garlic, fish, and other stinky-in-the-kitchen stuff.

❸ The most revolutionary new way to cook is with the NuWave Infrared Oven. It broils, roasts, grills, barbecues, fries, toasts, steams . . . all without fats or oils. Using a patented three-way combination of conduction, convection, and infared, this thing cooks without heating up the kitchen. How cool is that?! It cooks fifty percent faster, saving seventy percent of the energy that you'd use with a conventional oven. Can't lose with that equation, Ms. Domesticity. It's quick, easy, nutritious. The American Institute for Cancer Research is reporting that high-heat broiling and grilling cause meat and fish to produce high levels of cancer-causing compounds. This thing might be the answer. I don't know. It's worth a try, though. (**www.nuwaveoven.com**)

Hip Tip

Every retro Granny needs a vintage lawn glider for the backyard. I got a cool fire-engine red metal one at **www.torransmfgco.com** *These are the real deal, just like our own grandmas had.*

Retro Granny

Think back to the stuff you loved about your grandmother's house. In these mod times, lots of vintage goods are available online. There's just something about those fab vintage colors and materials that bring back the best memories of the good old days.

1. I adored those old aluminum tumblers: The ones that kept drinks extra frosty-cold and emanated ice clouds when they touched your lips. The same factory is still making them nowadays, with hand-turned spun aluminum in the original funky colors. (**www.alstos.com**) Click on "indoors" then "kitchen" to find the aluminum tumblers.

2. Retro Fiesta dinnerware is still around today too, manufactured in West Virginia by the Homer Laughlin China Co. Invented in 1936, Fiestaware became the most widely collected china in the world, and the line now incorporates fifteen spectacular colors in the boldest, brightest shades for contemporary kitchens. I love the scarlett red art deco plates, which make my kitchen feel ultra-hip. All lead-free, of course, Fiesta dinnerware will light up the table in any grandmother's kitchen. (**www.hlchina.com**)

3. The baby who's put on his back will spend a lot of time looking up at your ceilings, so get some reproduction tin-type ceilings. You can find these on the Internet, in any color imaginable. Speaking of colors, you can find the snazziest retro refrigerators at **www.bigchillfridge.com**. Retro red and orange and blue, oh, my! I have my eye on the fire engine red, which could actually excite me about going into my kitchen and pretending to be domestic.

Fixer of all Boo-Boos

You remember how it was: Grandma simply kissed the boo-boo with her wrinkled old lips, and it was instantly better. My Grammy made mint tea and buttered toast to make me feel better, and I always did. When Connor falls and bumps his knee, I have to kiss it on the hurting spot, just like every grandma in the history of the world. Now that you're a grandmother, be a crinkly-lipped healer, too.

1. Cover scrapes with bacon band-aids. Every grandmother has to have some cool band-aids. Perpetual Kid gives you a selection that includes Jesus, beef T-bone steaks, pirates, and sushi. The grandkid will be trying to bleed. just so he can be bandaged with these. (**www.perpetualkid.com**)

2. Make her some chicken soup and present it in the Tilted Soup Bowl. Created by a retired veteran, the bowl is angled so that a kid can eat soup without tipping the bowl. Niiiice. (**www.thetiltedsoupbowl.com**)

3. Serve the sick kid some hot cocoa or cold ginger ale in a personalized mug from **www.thestationerystudio.com**. This way you won't get sick too, because nobody will forget which cup the sick kid drank from.

Grandma Has a Bobbly Head

Laughter's the best medicine, so crack up your grandkid with a customized Bobblehead, starring - TA-DA - Grandma's head! Choose from lots of bodacious bodies, topped with a likeness of your face. We all start a little unwelcome head-bobbling as we age, anyway, so you might as well make it official with one of these fun Bobbleheads. (**www.headbobble.com**)

Doctor, Doctor, Give Me the News

Remember the doctor kits that your kids (and probably even you) played with? Well, they're still around. I got Connor a Fisher-Price doctor kit, and it's one of his favorite toys. "I doctor you, M'Mere," he says, and promptly listens to my heart, ("Not good," he states) takes my blood pressure, gives me a shot, looks in my ears ("Not good"), and slaps a band-aid across my wrist. He finishes the doctor visit by informing me—the patient—that I owe him—Doctor Connor—two dollars. Maybe someday he'll become a real doctor, thanks to me and Fisher-Price, and then he'll pay back his babysitting grandmother with a swimming pool or something.

Two things to always have in your medicine cabinet, in case of allergic reactions, are Benadryl and an EpiPen (check out **www.epipen.com** to learn about how and when to use it). Nowadays, allergies and asthma are on the rise. There's also been a huge increase in the number of kids who are allergic to peanuts and shrimp. Your doctor can write a prescription for the EpiPen; the Benadryl can be purchased in any pharmacy. It's also not a bad idea to learn CPR and the Heimlech maneuver. Becoming a grandmother brings out the doctor—or nurse—in us.

Poison Control

Find the number of your local Poison Control Center online at **www.keepkidshealthy.com**. The national number is **1-800-222-1222**. Keep that number on your fridge. Remember how we all kept a bottle of Syrup of Ipecac, used to induce vomiting in case of poisoning? That's no longer recommended. Lock your cupboards, keep cleaning products away from the rugrat, and you should be fine. Be aware that poinsettias are dangerous for little ones if consumed. You can do without those ugly red things at holiday time, can't you?

You Don't Want a Dirty Grandkid

There's nothing worse than a dirty grandkid. Remember how hippies smelled back in Woodstock times? Recall the smell of dreadlocks not washed for weeks? You so don't want the kid to smell like the good old days, so make bath time fun with this stuff:

1. Baby Scholars has a line of products like puppets and books for the bath, so you can multi-task and make them clean and smart at the same time. (**www.babyscholars.com**)

2. Amazon.com sells the original Mr. Bubble, and so do some stores. Sweet. It's fun to bathe the grandchild in the same brand of bubbles that we used as kids. Just be careful with bubble baths. Poison control gets thousands of calls about kids swallowing the stuff, and too much use can cause bladder problems, and that might just be worse than a dirty grandkid.

3. Decorate your bathroom in a theme that'll thrill the kid. Make sure you can live with it, too, unless you plan on being a dirty grandmother. (And there really is nothing worse than that.) Visit **www.kidsdecor.net** for theme bathroom décor that includes bugs, surfing, bumblebees, and cowboys. The cowboy kit includes western hat drawer pulls and a cactus toothbrush holder. YEE-HAW!

Hip Tip

Set the temperature of your hot water heater to 120 degrees Fahrenheit to prevent scalds.

A Grandma Needs
Really Great Sheets and Towels

Because the kid might occasionally be pulling an overnighter at your house, you need to have some first-rate sheets and towels. Throw in a couple of quality pillowcases too. It's a fine excuse to update your wretched linen closet. And while you're at it, toss in a quilt. Every grandmother has to own a quilt, or you might just be disowned by the club. Here are three places to shop:

1. **www.cuddledown.com**: For really soft flannel sheets. Admit it, you are so ready for flannel. It'll be just like sleeping on your 1980s shirts. Ahhhh! Flannel rules!

2. **www.toocooltshirtquilts.com**: For a quilt made from your old T-shirts. What a creative way to save those 1970s Rolling Stones and Fleetwood Mac shirts for all eternity! For an extra added touch, use some special baby T-shirts (from your kid and the grandkid) and outgrown kid clothes too. They'll be fighting over this one after you're dead.

3. **www.econatural.com**: For one hundred percent bamboo towels that contain no dye and are naturally antibacterial. You'll never want to get dressed, but you'd better do it. I'm not writing a page about the Nudist Grandma.

Let's Spend the Night Together

We who raised our kids with "the Family Bed" philosophy slept with our children until they entered kindergarten. It was easy, and cozy, and enjoyable. After all, that kid's going to hit an age where he wouldn't be caught dead in your bed, so why not enjoy the snuggling while you can? Connor sleeps with me on stayover nights, but his parents don't necessarily agree that's best. To each his own. Sleep is a personal thing. Families in other cultures consider co-sleeping to be beneficial for bonding, warmth, security, and space-saving. Some Americans disagree. It's a controversy, but what isn't these days? Go with your gut on this decision. Just be careful about sleeping with infants, especially if you're a heavy sleeper (or a heavy person). Nothing cute about rolling over and squishing your grandkid in the middle of the night.

Kids love sleeping bags, so get the little slumber monster a cool one for those essential sleepovers at your house. I got Connor a fab little cowboy bag at **www.bazoongi.com**. And get this: These bags come with a backpack, so the kid can tote it easily from house to house!

Get a little hippie sofa for the grandkid or the dog at **www.floociedoocie.com**. They have the best retro designs that'll remind you of that favorite dress from the '60s. Our golden retriever Angel relaxes on the Squiggles model, a swirly blue and purple design that I swear I remember seeing on Marcia Brady.

The Wacko Next Door

Sad, but this is one scary world. Check out the Web site **www.familywatchdog.us;** You type in your home address and then see pictures of all the registered sex offenders who live near you. I was astounded to see eleven creepy-as-hell monsters living near me, in conservative Lancaster County, Pennsylvania.

Discipline Tips

If you're a babysitting grandma, or hosting the kid overnight, you may need to discipline him sometimes. It doesn't mean you're the bad guy; it means that the kid needs to know he's done something wrong so he doesn't grow up to become a bad man. But don't spank him, Granny Dearest. Those days are over. Time out is the way to go: one minute per age (the child's age, not yours). For those very rare time out occasions (my grandson is an angel, you know), I use the sofa. No TV. No books or toys. Just him and the couch. It works just fine. Some people have exclusive spots that are used for nothing but time out; you can find ideas at **www.timeoutspots.com**. You can even try these for times when Grandpa needs some disciplne, though I doubt it'll work.

Story From a **Hip Grandma**

Funny Things My Granddaughter Said

When Charlotte was about 3 or 4, I took her into a ladies room in some restaurant.

She asked, "How old are you, Grammy?"

I said, "39."

She said, "That is the same age as my other grandmother!"

Charlotte and I were sitting in the back seat of the car.

I said, "I love your pretty dress."

Her reply, "Don't you like my pretty face?"

—Betsey Beamish
Hip Grandma
Pacific Palisades, CA

Toyboxes and the Stuff to Put in Them

So you thought that you had your house back. You assumed that there would be no more toyboxes in the living room. You assumed wrong. Even if you're not a regular babysitting grandma, you gotta have the toys and a place to keep them. You don't want to be a geeky granny, do you? The House With No Toys? No way. My ultimate goal is to turn my house into NeverLand, except without Michael Jackson.

1 For a big selection of awesome toy boxes with lids that won't fall on the kid's head, try **www.itoyboxes.com**.

2 Fill your toybox with treasures from **www.tinylove.com** and **www.alextoys.com**. These two companies offer award-winning, educational and art-happy toys that'll ensure playing in Granny's living room is really the making of a genius. Going through their catalogs reminds me of poring for hours over the Sears Wish Book back in the '60s. Pure toy lust. Another cool company (run by a grandmother!) is imagiPlay (**www.imagiPlay.com**). Spark imagination with these socially responsible, environmentally-friendly toys.

3 Don't forget to have some Crayola crayons on hand, Granny. Invented in 1903, these were your grandma's crayons—and they're still around today. Nowadays, Crayolas glitter, sparkle, glow in the dark, smell like flowers, wash off walls, and change colors. Wow. Crayons have come a long way since the days of eight colors. The factory's in Easton, Pa., and it's open for tours.

They Really Do Make 'Em Like They Used To!

Fill your Grandma House with classic toys like Slinky Dogs and Creepy Crawler Workshops and crates of plastic food, Bozo Bop Bags and Rock 'Em Sock 'Em Robots, Marvel The Mustang and Tinker Toys. Not only will the kid have a blast, but so will you. Some Web sites to check out for real retro are **www.backtobasicstoys.com** and **www.playthingspast.com**.

Don't forget to get a classic Flexible Flyer sled for snow days. Invented in 1889, the old wooden sled with red runners is still the hottest thing on snow today.

Oh, and remember Etch-A-Sketch? The Ohio Art company is still around, making mod Etch-A-Sketches and other updated art-encouraging goods. My favorite is Doodle Doug, who's kind of like the old Spirograph on spider speed. You can find Ohio Art online at **www.world-of-toys.com**.

It's a Dog Eat Baby World

Keep kids under the age of five away from turtles, lizards, and snakes. Salmonella is the risk with these critters, so if your grandchild touches one, wash his hands afterward. Also, if you're a dog owner, be aware that three breeds of dogs—Rottweilers, Pit Bulls, and German Shepherds—are responsible for fifty percent of the fatal dog bites in America. If you have a good dog, ease the canine slowly into the baby thing. Introduce dog to baby, and let him sniff. Give it time; this human creature is invading his territory, you know.

Think Outside the Box
about Your House:

My home isn't a magazine house. It's an eclectic house, packed with random stuff that I think is cool. My grandson seems to agree. Here are some ideas for you, Woman Of The House:

1. I personally think that every grandmother should have a cuckoo clock. It adds a little wacky excitement to the passing of time.

2. I grew up playing the guitar, and I hung guitar holders on the kitchen walls. My red 1969 Epiphone and my 1978 Alvarez acoustic enchant my grandson. If you played an instrument, and you still own it, think about hanging it on the wall or from the ceiling. We also have an ancient accordion, a piano, a drum kit, a keyboard, two bass guitars, an antique trumpet, and an old banjo. Nothing like surrounding your grandchild with music.

3. In my living room, I have a vintage Charlie Parker ventriloquist's puppet, a three-foot-tall Halloween witch, and a big framed print of retro Barnum & Bailey clowns. Connor's naptime ritual is to say "sweet dreams" to the puppet (the puppet says it in return), to wave to the witch (she doesn't wave back), and to kiss one of the clowns. I kiss one too. It's our naptime tradition. Every grandmother's house should have traditions.

4. My bathroom walls are covered with old album covers and records from my teen days, as well as with jewel cases from hundreds of CDs. Sheet music is glued to the ceiling, and my son's first toy guitar is glued on a wall. Behind the toilet is a John Lennon print and that famous shot of Bruce Springsteen's 1980s butt. If you have lots of album covers and records and CD cases, try hot-gluing them onto the walls. It looks very cool, and the grandkid will think so too.

⑤ Every grandmother's house needs a cookie jar. It's part of the Grandma's Code of Home Ethics. Scope the local flea markets for vintage collectible jars, or go online. Target and Wal-Mart and other discount stores have them, and so do upscale places like Macy's and Bloomingdales. The cookie jar will live forever in the grandkid's memories, and one day maybe she'll inherit it for her own grandkids.

We Shall Overcome
by Fostering Multiculturalism

We who grew up in the days of race riots and prejudice know how ugly that stuff can get. Encourage acceptance, understanding, and equality with politically-correct toys that encompass all races and nationalities. I never had a black baby doll, and maybe you never did either. Your grandkid should. America is a melting pot, and we WASP-ish types need to make sure that our white-bread grandkids know that.

I Love You More. No, I Love You More

This book includes a lot of yada-yada about material goods, because that stuff is fun and a lot of us love to shop. It's an estrogen thing. However, don't forget that the goods do not a grandma make. It's really about the stuff you can't touch: love. The invisible magic that bonds you like Super Glue to this new little human that you'd walk through snakes to save. Love is really all that matters, and plenty of it will make you not only hip, but happy. Shine on, sister, and get the book "I Love You More" at **www.hippieandthebaldchick.com**. It's a sweet tribute to that mystical thing that makes the world go 'round: the groovy kind of love shared by you and the kid.

Profound Question

"How do you feel when people are mean to you?" I asked. It was one of those rare "teachable moments." My five year old grandson and I were sitting on the porch swing, enjoying a warm spring day. I had his undivided attention (or so I thought), so I seized the opportunity to discuss a subject I'd been wanting to bring up at just the right time.

"I don't like it," was his predictable reply -- just what I'd hoped he would say. I explained that others feel that same way when he's unkind to them.

To my delight, he seemed to be listening for a change. He pursed his lips and stared at me in silence with wide eyes.

"If you don't share your toys with other boys, they will feel sad," I continued. Cobi appeared to concentrate on my words, ruminating over them like a cow chewing its cud.

"And if you don't take turns on the swing, other kids might not want to play with you." He squinted his eyes, wrinkled his brow, and scratched his head. I knew he was soaking up my wisdom like a sponge. I was thrilled that he didn't respond with the usual arguments like, "But graaaaaaama, when I tripped Robert, he didn't get hurt," or "Haley likes it when I take her ball."

Pleased with myself and the way my lecture was going, I summed it up with the golden rule. "We need to treat other people the same way we like to be treated," I explained. "That way, things will go more smoothly and everyone will be happier." Satisfied that I had conveyed this important lesson to him, and that he'd taken it so well, I concluded my discourse by asking if he had any questions.

"Yeah," he replied enthusiastically. "Why don't bugs have ears, and do they ever sneeze?"

—Marsha Jordan
Author of "Hugs, Hope, and Peanut Butter"
www.hugsandhope.org/pb.htm

Hip Grandma Fashion

chapter 4

Robes and Slippers and Snuggly Fleece Blankets

Every good grandmother needs a cool and crazy robe and slippers, for those snazzy sleepovers and shivery winter nights. Forget the skimpy Victoria's Secret, sweetie. That ship has sailed, and I'm afraid that it's not coming back. Whip up some hot chocolate: the gourmet dark chocolate fancy kind from **www.omanhene.com**. Rent some DVDs. Put some logs on the fire, or just crank up the heater. Snuggle with the grandkid for a cozy time on a cold winter's night. Here are the essentials:

1. A plush robe from Barefoot Dreams for you, and a CozyChic Hoodie for the grandkid. These are Oprah's favorite robes, and you're sure to love them too. (**www.barefootdreams.com**)

2. Matching theme jammies and slippers from Crazy For Bargains. You could put the grandkid in pigs, and you dress in the cow pattern. Or vice versa. Whatever. Just make it a pajama party she'll never forget. (**www.crazyforbargains.com**) Check out **www.pajamaprogram.org**, and help buy jammies and books for kids who are waiting to be adopted. Every child deserves a good tucking-in, so help someone less fortunate than your coddled grandkid.

3. A wildlife fleece throw blanket from Frosty Fleece. Get one with a pattern that conceals spilled hot chocolate and marshmallow globs from the smores you're sure to make (**www.frostyfleece.com**). And get the kid his own cozy little fleece, personalized with his name, from Baby Be Hip. (**www.babybehip.com**)

Hip Tip

*This one is a no-brainer: Get a couple packs of Tot Finder stickers, so your precious little one can be easily located by firefighters in the event of a fire. (**www.totfinder.com**)*

For the Little Bit of Punk in You

If you ever listened to the Ramones or the Sex Pistols, you know you've got it: a little bit of punk. Be an old-school punk granny who'll still be in fashion with this anti-establishment, DIY stuff for the sub-culture:

1. Converse sneakers: Custom design a pair of hardcore Chuck Taylors personalized with your grandma name, and then make a matching pair for your soon-to-be-questioning-authority little punker. (**www.converse.com**)

2. Baby Rock Star shirts: From rock to punk, they've got it all. Rock on! (**www.babyrockstar.com**)

3. The Punk Farm book: Old McDonald gone punk. EEE-I-EEE-I-OH!! Everybody scream it!! You'll wanna be sedated after reading this one a dozen times. (**www.punkfarm.com**)

Tats for Tots

Little ones are crazy for fake tattoos, so you might as well educate them while pressing temporary designs onto their skin. The site **www.tattoosfortots.com** spells out the word of the design, so that the tiny tattooed ones learn spelling without even realizing it.

If You're a New-Age Old Lady

All those "Bewitched" shows and Ouija Boards took their toll. We believe in magic. Twitch your nose if you're the kind of grandma who's into new-age. Here's the scoop on some *Twilight Zone* whoo-whoo for you.

1. Nirup, a spiritual advisor/psychic reader, lives in the red rocks of Sedona, Arizona. You know, the vortex spiritual center of the U.S. Nirup is the real deal. No fake psychic crap here. She'll read your voice's good vibrations over the phone. She'll know things about that lovely baby, and she'll give some life advice worth following. (**www.psychicnirup.com**)

2. Heaven's Child is a great Web site with free horoscopes for the kid, showing caregivers from the Age of Aquarius how to best entertain a child with help from energies swirling from the stars. (**www.heavenschild.com.au**)

3. Pyramid Collection has a gorgeous Neptune Mystic Topaz Ring guaranteed to emanate cooling, soothing bling-bling peace to the kid in your presence. Even if that's a crock, the set-in-silver ring is beautiful and blue and sure to enchant both you and the child. (**www.pyramidcollection.com**)

Fancy yourself *a fairy, a pirate, or a rock-and-roll gypsy kind of chick—Gypsy Moon has romantic clothing that fits real women, with lots of velvet and silk and ruffles and such. (www.gypsymoon.com)*

Hats Are for Grannies

Eat your heart out, Red Hat Society. We of The Hip Grandmas Club out-cool you any day. Eat our dust. Kiss our butts. We ROCK! And we don't need no stinkin' red hats. Here are the official hats of The Hip Grandmas Club, all to be found at **www.hotilids.com.** (They agree with us that our heads are the hottest part of our bods, so we just couldn't help but love 'em.)

1 For hip grandmothers of one grandkid: the Striped Newsie with Flower Pin.

2 For hip grandmothers of two grandkids: The hip hand-crocheted Skull Cap. This is not your grandmother's crochet, ladies. Can you say "Uber-Cool, Yo?" These can be customized with your own embellishments.

3 For hip grandmothers of three or more grandkids: the Cowgirl Hat. Whether you choose the patch leather, an animal print, or a straw cowgirl with a pink dahlia, you'll be standing tall. One benefit of the Cowgirl Hat is that it's big enough to cover the bald spots, gray patches, and white streaks that grandmothers of three (or more) are prone to acquiring. It also casts a nice shadow upon those bags under your eyes and the saggy skin on your neck. Remember the late Freddie Prinz of the TV show "Chico and the Man"? As Freddie said, you'll be "Looook-ing gooooood."

For Beautiful Skin
and Hair Below that Hat

We of the Coppertone generation need a little skin help, ladies. I myself worshiped the sun from my aluminum foil tanning mat. Yikes! I also did the baby oil, the Sun-In on the hair (wicked orange streaks–look out!), and the tanning beds. Oh, the tanning beds. When I think back to all the tanning I did, I consider myself lucky that my face hasn't turned into an alligator purse.

1. The biggest miracle in machines that reincarnate a more youthful you is the new explosion in photo rejuvenation. Girlfriends, these things are magic. I used the Quasar Baby for seven weeks, and my face went back in time at least seven years. The light reduces crow's feet, laugh lines, frown lines, shrinks pores, eliminates age spots, and diminishes scars and inflammation. (**www.cosmeticlight.com**)

2. The coolest conditioner for hair of any length is Wen by Chaz Dean. Remember that smell your own grandmother had? Kind of like a combination of old-lady skin, hair that hadn't been washed since the last perm, peppermint candies, and powder? You don't want to smell like that. With Wen, you'll waft deliciously of figs, cucumbers or almonds: fresh and clean. It's a bit pricey, but you're worth it. (**www.chazdean.com**)

3. Don't have a granny face. Our grandmothers used lard, and we ourselves once faithfully attended the Church of Oil of Olay, but that's old school. One of the best skin prescriptions I've found is from Renée Rouleau. Renée learned her stuff from hanging out in her own grandmother's beauty salon, and she's formulated products that combine the best of science and nature. Never tested on animals, this stuff will have your skin shouting Hallelujah. (**www.reneerouleau.com**)

Every Old Barn Looks Better With Some New Paint

Treat yourself to some great new makeup, because inside every old grandma is a little girl who loves to paint her face. Some of the hippest places to shop:

1. Duwop, where the name takes you back to your birth year. They have an antibacterial pencil sharpener so you don't ruin those bifocaled eyes any worse than you already have. (**www.duwop.com**)

2. Cargo, whose biodegradable lipstick cartons are totally da bomb. (**www.cargocosmetics.com**)

3. Stila, where you can order stuff good enough for the celebs. (**www.stilacosmetics.com**)

3 Things Not To Say To Your Non-Grandma Friends:

"Look at these pictures! And *these* pictures! And these, and these, and these!"

"I don't have time for lunch. Maybe never again will I have time for lunch."

"Awwww; smell my hands! I smell like baby! I just changed the baby! Don't I smell like baby?!"

Hair Today, Gone Tomorrow

Leg hair growth slows as we age, leaving more time to tweeze that stubborn chin and moustache growth. There's no excuse for having a beard or a moustache, Grandma, except the one that involves working with a circus sideshow. For the sake of grandmothers everywhere, get rid of facial hair. Any local spa can do it.

What a Babe: Grandmom-Hattan

Okay; so you're never going to look 25 again. Or 30.
Or, sorry to inform you, 35. It's all right. Those Barbie dolls of
our childhood were so fake. Wisdom comes with age. Your brains
are what matter, and you can bring home the bacon and fry it up
in a pan. You don't really care about your looks anyway, now that
you're the Grandma. Screw Jessica Simpson and her toddler-sized
hot pants. You don't care if you never look like that again.
Well, maybe just a little . . .

1. Brighten up that yellow old granny grin at Brite Smile.
   I went to the one in Manhattan, and it felt like a spa for my
   teeth. Like Carly Simon says: You're so vain. Whiten your
   teeth. I bet you think this book is about you, don't you?
   Don't you? Don't you? (**www.britesmile.com**)

2. While you're in the city (Grandmom-Hattan), you might as
   well catch a cab and head on over to the John Barrett salon,
   up on the top of Bergdorf Goodman. Barrett created the
   haircuts for the show "Friends." Now, there's no guarantee
   that you're going to walk out of there looking like Courtney
   Cox, but he works with what you give him.

3. Get your unibrow (or chin) tweezed at the Gemini salon,
   down in the West Village. Greenwich is where all the cool
   people hang, ya know? Hipsters. Including you. The woman
   with the white teeth, good hair, and nice eyebrows. What a
   babe. (**www.geminisalonnyc.com**)

Friends Don't Let
Friends Wear Grandma Jeans

Don't wear jeans up around your waist. Don't wear granny panties. Don't wear red sweatshirts embroidered with your grandkids' names or with Christmas pictures. Don't wear button cardigans or T-shirts with wildlife photographs. Please. Don't. For the sake of grandmas everywhere.

Grandma's Feet

Remember Granny's feet? The bunions and the corns and the hammertoes? Oh, you so don't want those. Cure hammertoes with Yoga Toes from Yoga Pro (**www.yogapro.com**). Remember how you wore those spiked heels back in your sexy-shoe days? They weren't good for your feet. Orthopedic surgeon Taryn Rose has designed a happenin' line of hot shoes that don't sacrifice sexy for safe. Padding is made from a trademarked material called Poron, a super-foam developed by NASA. Hand-crafted in Italy with three hours of stitching put into each shoe, these babies are made of the best butter-soft leather under the sun. They're a bit pricey, but aren't your feet worth it? Designed especially for baby boomers like you, these shoes will make you feel like you're walking on the moon. (**www.tarynrose.com**)

You Can Dress 'Em Up and Take 'Em Anywhere

For those snazzy special occasions, gussy your grandkids in better-than-Sunday-best, bought by Ms. Extravagant Grandma especially for her little angel eyes. Penguins are popular now, so put your grandson in a dapper tuxedo from **www.friartux.com** or **www.nanasboutique.com**. For the little princess, check out **www.gingerpye.com** or **www.tuttibella.com**. Go all-out if the event is a christening or a wedding or a confirmation. For normal days that include playing, make sure your grand one is the best dressed baby in the sandbox by ordering something from **www.sandboxcouture.com**. Rationalize your splurge by finding your own clothes at Goodwill, TJ Maxx, Target, or the local yard sale. It's all about priorities, baby.

One, Two, Buckle My Shoe

The newest medical research says that barefoot is best. That, however, isn't always practical or safe, so the next best thing is to get some shoes from **www.preschoolians.com**. They've been featured on the Today Show, and they're so not yesterday. Billed as "the most flexible shoes in the world," these kickers are cool.

Little, Black, and Hip

Popularized by designer Coco Chanel in the 1920s, the Little Black Dress is one wardrobe essential that no grandmother should be without. It's simple, slimming, stunning, and so chic, Woman of the Evening. Little black dresses may be found all over this land as well as all over the Web, and check out **www.thatperfectlittleblackdress.com** for vintage dresses. They not only have retro dresses from varied eras, but they have Little Black Hats, Little Black Purses, Evening Coats, and Patterns for those daring enough to sew their own Little Black Dress. For those who don't man (or woman) the sewing machine, check out **www.littleblackdressshop.com** for everything from casual to cocktail, with all the bling-bling you'll need. Ooh, la, la . . . you're back in black!

Remember your *grandmother's stockings? The ones with the straight seam down the back of the leg? Well, they're hip once again, and so are fishnets and crocheted thigh-highs and socks of every stripe and color. Check out www.stockingirl.com and www.joyofsox.com for some fashionable feet frenzy, Funky One.*

What Not To Wear (The Grandma Version)

It's a balancing act, this dressing the grandmother business. You don't want to be a dork, and you don't want to look like a porker. You don't want to look like a slut, and you don't want the world to see your granny butt. You still want to be cool, but you don't want to look like a fool. What's a hip grandma to do?

DO NOT **Wear:**

1. Granny panties. Any waistband—elastic or otherwise—that touches your bellybutton is not good. Also, do not wear thongs. Do not wear thongs. Repeat that over and over.

2. No jeans with straight legs, no high waists, no distressed 1980s tie-dye with zippers or lace or safety pins on the sides.

3. Shirts that expose your belly button. We know that you have one. Don't show it. Please.

4. Hot pants. Short shorts. Tight skirts. Tight shirts. Lycra. Your aerobic tights from 1985. The sweat pants that say Hot Stuff on the butt.

5. Birkenstocks with socks.

6. The Catholic girl knee-socks and plaid skirt ensemble.

7. Your 1970s pink plaid bellbottoms.

8. Anything from the 1980s, especially the orange ruffled fluorescent dress.

9. Your husband's T-shirts, unless you're heading to the gym and nowhere else. And even then, no shirts that advertise condoms or Nascar or beer.

10. Teacher dresses with pictures of primary-color dinosaurs and dogs.

Check out these three virtually great places to shop:

www.newport-news.com • www.whiteandblack.com
www.bostonproper.com

**And for stores? One word: Chico's. They're also online at
www.chicos.com**

DO **Wear:**

1 Jeans that flatter your shape. Flared leg; slightly low waist; not too tight. You should be able to sit without a split and bend without a bare back end.

2 Shirts that cover most of your boobs and all of your belly.

3 Shoes that are comfy and not too ugly, without any duct tape patches.

4 Workout clothes that are suitable for the grocery store as well as the gym or Yoga studio. No hot-pink Spandex shorts, please.

5 Longer shorts and Capris. These make you look like a non-sleaze, and are easy to move in.

6 Dresses that are cool and funky. Fairy hems are good, and so are maxis and knee-length and calf-length.

7 Bras that hold everything as tightly as your first boyfriend did.

8 Panties that control the jiggle while maintaining the wiggle.

9 Long jackets and sweaters that make you look like a lean, mean, Granny machine.

10 Mod suits with tailored pants and jackets that are not too stuffy or fluffy, and hippie skirts that make you flow like Stevie Nicks.

The Hip Grandma
On the Road

chapter 5

A Grandma Car: NOT!

Just because you're a grandmother doesn't mean that you need to drive a Grandma Car. Forget the stereotypical big Buick, or the wood-grained station wagon. True Confession: I used to drive a minivan, back when there were little kids in the house. The Ninnyvan, as I so affectionately called her, was the typical MomVan: boring, bland, blah. Two years ago, I acquired what I think of as the perfect car for any grandmother: a PT Cruiser. She's cool, curvy, compact yet roomy, and purple. She has peace signs and John Lennon bumper magnets, and sexy chrome wheels with a lot of shine. Plummie works just fine for the grandkid: It's easy to retrieve him from the backseat, as PT Cruisers are four-door cars. This isn't an ugly four-door car, though. This is a hot car for any cool grandmotherly chick. She's sturdy and safe and fairly easy on the gasoline bill. Sweet. I think I've just named PT Cruiser as the official car of The Hip Grandmas Club. Hey, maybe they'll give me a discount on my next car?!

Hip Tip

Don't hang one of those stupid Baby On Board signs in your car window. What do you think—that eighteen-wheeler isn't going to crash into you, just because the driver reads the sign and thinks, "Oh, I guess I won't hit this one. There's a baby on board." I also don't like "God Is My Co-Pilot." That's a scary thought, that the grandmother is the pilot and the Higher Power is the second-in-command. Yikes.

Keeping the Grandkid
Safe (And Quiet) in the Car

Of course, you're an excellent driver. But so was the character in "Rain Man." Accidents happen. Sometimes they're the fault of other people. Sometimes not. Keep the precious cargo safe and protected and content with this on-the-go stuff.

A car seat by SafeGuard is a good place to start. They make the most advanced car seat in the world, and it comes in four go-with-anything colors. (**www.safeguardseat.com**) Called a "revolutionary breakthrough" by iParenting.com, this is a child seat that'll make you feel good about driving. And if you're thinking about just transferring the seat from the kid's parents' car to your car every time you take him somewhere, forget about it. It's not worth the hassle. Get your own, cheapo. Combi makes a great booster car seat for the non-baby. (**www.combi-intl.com**) Sunshine Kids also makes a great seat. (**www.skjp.com**)

Now that the kid is safe, keeping him quiet and happy is a whole other ball game, girlfriend. Music can help. Toys attached to the car seat are good for teeny ones. Playing games as you drive works with the older set. ("Where's a cow? What color is it? Find me a green tree. Good. Now find a . . . pink flower! Okay. Can you see a . . . chicken? Find me a chicken! Excellent. Now how about a red barn? Do you see a horse? I do! I see a horse! Whoops; Grandma needs to look at the road now, sweetie. No, I can't turn around. Find me a . . . nap!")

When traveling with children, it's a good idea to be prepared for emergencies. After hearing of a turnpike traffic jam in which people were stuck for seven hours (on a summer day), I decided that I should always have a few diapers, food, and drink while transporting the Con-Man. A recent three inches of snow with a frosting of ice stranded hundreds of people on a Pennsylvania highway for more than twenty-four hours. Two freaking days sitting in a line of vehicles on a road, running out of gas and having to pee in front of truck drivers. Ohmigod. That's the

Highway To Hell. After hearing that news, I decided that in addition to the necessary snacks and drinks, any grandmother worth her salt is going to keep a big empty cup in the car. You know, for peeing in private rather than along the side of the road? Our bladders ain't what they used to be, you know. Be prepared.

Story From a **Hip Grandma**

The Sound of Music

My rour-year old grandson has always had a fascination with my ukulele. It's just an inexpensive one that I bought to try to play, and I have let the grandchildren play it often. One afternoon as I was doing something in my room, Haden came in and asked if he could play my "little guitar." I got it out for him, he went into the living room and I went back to whatever it was I was doing. A few minutes later I heard blood-curdling screaming coming from the living room. I rushed out of my room to see what had happened, and there was Haden just standing there with the ukulele. I was looking for signs of some horrendous accident and asked him what was wrong. He looked at me with a confused and possibly a little hurt expression and said, "I was SINGING!"

—Linda Dust
Hip Grandma

On the Beach, Baby

Yeah, yeah, so you hate to wear a swimsuit. Maybe you're in the quintessential black one-piece, or it might have even worsened to the stage where you're sporting the geeky little skirt on your not-so-cute dimpled bottom. Even if you're not in bikini shape, get yourself out on the sand and into the waves. Build castles. Boogie board. Jump waves. Dig for crabs. Just don't be one. Life is a beach!

1. Can You Dig It? The ultimate castle-making kit that'll have you sculpting castles fit for a queen. The Super Deluxe kit has everything you need to star on the sand. You'll be an expert in no time, building intricate detailed sand castles that make people stop and point. It'll be nice to have them noticing the fancy castle, rather than the way your pudgy granny gut hangs over the top of your swimsuit bottom. These castles outshine the floppiest cellulite thighs, so nobody will notice you're no longer Cheryl Tiegs-ish on the beach. (**www.canyoudigit.com**)

2. Get your own hut or beach cabana from **www.shadeusa.com**. Shade that precious skin (not yours, hers!) and avoid burns. Nothing like sun poisoning to harsh your mellow. Maybe you could borrow a hot cabana boy to fetch your drinks and rub lotion on those hard-to-reach spots in the middle of your back. Feed the seagulls, even if the beach police say not to, because it's really fun. Nothing like the swoop of a Cheetos-lusting gull to make the grandkid giggle. Protect your head. Seagull poop in your hair harshes the mellow even quicker than sunburn.

3. The best beach town in the U.S.A. (IMHO) is Ocean Grove, New Jersey. It's clean, quiet (a dry town, so no drunk college kids here), Victorian, and non-commercialized. No tacky T-shirt joints or arcades. (**www.albatrosshotel.net**)

Take a Trip to Amish Land

I live here, so Amishland is sorta boring to me. You'll like it, though, and your grandkid will be fascinated by encounters with people clad entirely in black (Amish, not Goths) who have no TVs, DVDs, computers, Xboxes, iPods, cars, or hairdryers. Ohmigod! So what is there to do in Lancaster County, Pennsylvania? Here are three of the best options:

1. Strasburg Railroad: America's oldest short-line railroad, with authentically restored passenger cars pulled by a coal-burning steam locomotive. Choo-Choo! Strasburg sometimes even hosts the rock star of trains: Thomas the Tank Engine. (**www.strasburgrailroad.com**) If you're staying overnight, check out the Red Caboose Motel, where you can sleep in an antique train car. (**www.redcaboosemotel.com**)

2. Dutch Wonderland: One of the coolest old amusement parks in the U.S. Their Happy Hauntings Halloween event is non-scary and kiddo-friendly, and their Winter Wonderland event is breath-taking, with real reindeer and sparkly lights.

3. HersheyPark: This one's about an hour from the heart of Amish country, but well worth the drive. Be sure to tour the chocolate factory while you're there. You can also ride the carousel, and the bumper cars, and the spiffy new roller coasters. But don't ride the old wooden one called the Wildcat. I broke my rib on that one, maybe because I am, um, a grandmother, with brittle old bones. But maybe not. (**www.hersheypa.com**)

Ghosts of Gettysburg

If you go to Hershey, you might as well get psyched to drive another hour and hit Gettysburg. It's a ghostly and historic place: educational for the grandkid and for you. There are loads of charming B&Bs in town, and narrated tours of the battlefields. Don't split until you've stayed overnight in one. The Battlefield B&B is my fave. An 1809 stone farmhouse surrounded by a pond (full of croaking somethings), a field with a lovely horse and pony, and a big old barn, it's the perfect place for your grandkids to learn about Civil War history. Costumed employees serve breakfast and give lectures (nice lectures, not mean ones). My son Zach was allowed to "shoot" the Civil War cannon several years ago when we stayed there. Is the Inn haunted? Ah-hem. That's for me to know, and for you to find out. (**www.gettysburgbattlefield.com**)

Hip Grandma Lois Syzmanski and her homegirl Shelley Sykes have written a spooky series of ghost stories for kids called "The Gettysburg Ghost Gang." Try reading them in the room at night, if you dare. Get ready for nightmares. While you're on the book kick, check out Linda Oatman High's *The Cemetery Keepers of Gettysburg*. (I know, I know. I have no pride.) Based on the real story of Elizabeth Thorn, who buried more than one hundred soldiers while six-months pregnant, *The Cemetery Keepers of Gettysburg* will educate, entertain, and inspire your little Gettysburg scholar. Read it, and then visit the Evergreen Cemetery. Expect chills.

Snack Attack

Load up with travel snacks to save money and keep blood-sugar levels at an even keel. Some of my favorites are Uncrustables (the no-crust peanut butter and jelly sandwiches from Smuckers), GoGurt (drinkable yogurt), and granola bars. If you have a tiny tot, don't forget the sippie cup. Pack plenty of wipes, changes of clothing, car entertainment, and diapers . . . for the grandkid, not for you.

Catching Some Air on the Slopes

Drive to the nearest ski resort and get your butt on the chair lift. Ski, snowboard, snowshoe, or drink coffee in the lodge. Your grandkid will be so friggin' proud of you, even if you just make it down the bunny slope without falling. I have a primo powder-blue Morrow snowboard with a lotus flower on it. (**www.morrow snowboards.com**) It's ever so girly, and I have the boots to match! Now if only I could learn how to ride the thing.

1. The coolest place east of the Mississipi—no contest—for family snow fun is Smugglers' Notch, Vermont. It's a happenin' place. The kids will never be bored and neither will you. The condos have dishwashers and washer/dryers so you can feel as if you're in your own kitchen, homegirl. Smugglers' is an environmentally-conscious business, so you can feel all peace, love, and granola about being there. This place is as good as Disney, Grandma, except with snow, skis, and fireplaces. They're open year-round, with fair-weather fun too. (**www.smuggs.com**)

2. Don't mortify the grandkid by wearing your old, torn bib overalls from 1975. Things have changed, darlin'. I bought some ski clothes from Betty Rides. They have a hot seat, insulated pockets, and a crotch gusset. I don't know what that is, but it scares me. Nonetheless, the clothes are stylin', cool, and they keep me really warm, which is important because I'm wimpy. Check them out at **www.bettyrides.com**. Another cool place for ski clothes is **www.orageski.com**.

3. Get your own snowshoes, and some for the little ones too. When it's not snowing, they look good hanging from the ceiling. When it is snowing, you can walk to the post office in them and watch reactions from the corner of your eye. (**www.redfeather.com**)

Born to Ski Wild

You can start your grandkids skiing at the age of one, using learning packages and Happy Skis designed by former U.S. ski champ Steve Lathrop. Steve believes that tots can ski independently by the age of two. (They may even be better than you, Grandma.) Check it out at **www.kid-ski.com.**

Be sure to keep the little one warm enough, because once the kid gets cold, it's all over. You can find the most rockin' little ski jackets on the slopes at **www.spyder.com,** and the most innovative gloves and mittens at **www.lbow.com.** Designed by a Minnesota mother of four who knows all about Snow-Packed-Wrist Syndrome, L-Bow offers long-arm gloves that extend all the way to the elbow. How cool is that for keeping the kids warm? You can find the best little fleece hats at **www.turtlefur.com.**

Grand Quotes

"No cowboy was ever faster on the draw than a grandparent pulling a baby picture out of a wallet."

~Author Unknown

"My grandkids believe I'm the oldest thing in the world. And after two or three hours with them, I believe it, too."

~Gene Perret

"If nothing is going well, call your grandmother."

~Italian Proverb

"A grandmother is a mother who has a second chance."

~Author Unknown

"Being pretty on the inside means you don't hit your brother and you eat all your peas - that's what my grandma taught me."

~Lord Chesterfield

If the Grandkid Lives Far Away

If the grandkid lives far away and you hardly ever get to see him despite your best attempts, do not despair. This is life in the twenty-first century. That is why we have airplanes: to fly grandmothers to visit their grandkids. Don't let money be an issue that keeps you from the grandkids. Even if you only see your little angel once or twice a year, there are ways to connect. Be there or be square.

1. Be kind of like a pirate, but without the wooden leg and eye patch. Send a message in a bottle. Combining Old World tradition with new innovation, a company called Timeless Message ships the coolest bottles with your sentiments sealed inside. It arrives on the grandkid's step in an awesome wooden crate. Their most popular bottle for grandmoms is the heart-shaped luminous red Corazon, hand-crafted in Europe. (**www.timelessmessage.com**)

2. Get a cell phone with unlimited weekend and evening minutes. Call the kid a lot, even when she can't yet talk. The sound of your voice will become familiar, and the baby will be less prone to screaming in fear when she finally sees you. When the kid is over five, it's time to start with the emails and the IM thing. Learn the acronyms—lol, l8r, wu, ttyl. Use them. nbd. lmao.

3. Make videos of yourself reading books, playing in the leaves, building a snowman, jumping into a pool. Talk to the kid as if he were there with you. Don't forget to make plans for a getaway at least once every year, so that you don't become known as the Invisible Grandma. Ghost grannies are so not cool. Life is short; they grow up too fast. Don't miss it.

Go West, Cowgirl

Okay, so I'm an East Coast girl. I love New York, and Philly, and even Jersey. But I love the West Coast too, so here are some places closer to the Pacific that'll make great getaways for you and the little cowpoke. (The buff cowboy Casanovas might cook something good on the campfire. Cool beans.) We who grew up on *The Lone Ranger* and *Gunsmoke* find that these western retreats bring back good old memories of horses and leather and Michael Landon, Sr. Dig out your cowgirl hats and blue jeans, and get ready for the ride of your life at a dude ranch vacation that the grandkid will never forget.

1. Colorado's Deer Valley Ranch offers activities for children and teens, and their staff of fifty works hard to ensure satisfied guests. In the same family since 1954, you can count on Deer Valley to give you a Rocky Mountain dude ranch experience that can't be beat with a stick. (**www.deervalleyranch.com**)

2. Nestled along Wyoming's Wind River, the Triangle C Ranch has one of the most famous children's programs in the U.S. (**www.trianglec.com**)

3. A working cattle ranch on three thousand acres of Arizona land, the White Stallion Ranch blends rugged Western informality with all the comforts of a fine resort. Oh, give me a home where the buffalo roam, and the deer and the antelope play. Where seldom is heard a discouraging word, and the massage can be scheduled each day. (**www.wsranch.com**)

You've Got Mail

Every kid loves getting mail, especially now that real hard-copy snail mail is becoming extinct. The Web site **www.surprisingkids.com** has fun stuff to send to your grandchild's mailbox.

Pack Your Bags: Cool Travel Gear

You're going to need some mod travel gear for all these trips. Don't mortify the grandkid by toting your old no-wheels brown leather bag complete with Captain and Tennille stickers from 1978. A tote with the Rolling Stones famous tongue logo is no longer hip, and neither is the carry-on with a laminated photo of Bobby Sherman's from the pages of Tiger Beat Magazine. Get with it, girl.

1. I got an ultra-light aqua-colored International Traveler wheeled suitcase from the pack-your-bag pros at **www.luggagepros.com**. When the thing is empty, I can literally lift it with one finger! When it's packed . . . Well, that's another story, one that could possibly involve carpal tunnel syndrome or the tenacious tendonitis. However, a heavy bag is a good way to get some hot young guy who resembles Johnny Depp or Orlando Bloom to carry the bag for Grandma. Can you say "Dirty Old Lady?"

2. Plane Quiet noise reduction headphones will mute the sounds of other people's annoying grandchildren. To find a Plane Quiet headset, click on "Headsets and Ear Phones" on **www.protravelgear.com**.

3. Block out light and look Hollywood with eye masks from **www.dreamessentials.com**. The leopard print or silk are sexy; unless you're driving, of course. Nothing cute about a dead grandmother. These eye masks evoke images of Marilyn Monroe.

Have Some Mace Face, Space Case

If it's just you and the grandkids, pack some protection. (No, I don't mean condoms. No use for those anymore, old lady.) I mean pepper spray, in case some space case is looking dangerous in a deserted parking lot. Spray his face with Mace; kick him where it counts; run like the dickens; scream your head off. Don't forget to take the kids with you as you're running. There's a lot of cool pepper spray on the market, cleverly disguised as lipstick cases and other innocuous stuff. Get some.

It's also good to have one of those portable alarms on hand— the kind that squeals when you pull the cord. Oh, and your cell phone. Keep it in your pocket, and make sure it's not dead. Being safe in this crazy world is important, especially when you have the little people to protect. It's no longer just self-defense; it's the safety of the most important little humans in the universe. Don't screw around in parking lots or garages, searching futilely for the keys through your mess of a handbag. Have those keys in your hand, with the biggest one stuck point-out between the index and second finger. This makes a great weapon, if needed. Practice your knee-in-the-groin move; you know, the one that you learned from Kate Jackson on *Charlie's Angels*— Pretend you're Cat Woman, even if you don't look quite as good in the black bodysuit.

Rain, Rain, Don't Go Away

The Carpenters had it wrong: Rainy days and Mondays aren't so bad after all. Raincoats nowadays are not the boring old yellow of our past. Check out **www.rainydaywear.com** for the best selection of groovy raincoats, umbrellas, and boots. Even Barbara Walters and *The View* dig this stuff that makes you wish for drizzle!

The PT Granny

Where are the trains? Where are the buses? Where are the ferries? This was the mantra beating deep in my heart for more than forty years after moving away from Staten Island in New York City.

Now my city is Mountain View, California. Its rural life, once based upon apricot and cherry orchards, is gone. Mountain View is now a busy Silicon Valley haven for fast moving electronics wizards and hard working business and service people. It lies south of San Francisco on the peninsula that makes up South San Francisco Bay. And guess what? I once again am blessed with the kind of public transportation (PT) that so enriched my childhood. As a grandmother that loves to teach, and with three curious-as-kittens grandchildren, I have begun to share with them the abundance of adventure, social exposure, life lessons, wonder, and joy that PT has to offer.

On Friday afternoons, my two older grandchildren come for an overnight. They are five and three-and-a-half years old. After they've played with my two cats, had a snack and gone potty (an absolute must in PT prep) we head out to catch the 3:12 bus at the covered bus stop on Castro Street. Just waiting for the bus is fun because of all the questions about sights, sounds, and other people. The conversation is electric. When the bus is spotted, the children erupt with joy. Do you know we have yet to have a bus driver, woman or man, who has not been delighted to hear the children say: "Hello Mr./Ms. Bus Driver," when getting on the bus and "Thank you, Mr./Ms. Bus Driver," upon getting off—I think we make their day. We ride only four stops. And yes, if I forget to pre-settle who will pull the cord, they do argue a little bit—but that's nothing.

When we get off the bus we are at the Mountain View Train Station. What an exciting classroom it is. Two different kinds of trains, diesel and electric, rush and glide to a halt. My grandchildren refer to them as "the noisy train" and "the quiet train." But if asked, they can name the trains by the type of power they use. Sometimes we just watch and listen at the station. The light down the tracks grows larger and larger, the clang of the warning bells shocks the air, the electric gate moves down and up, the red lights flash. All kinds and shapes of people rush off buses onto trains, off trains onto buses, and into cars. The passengers and the engineer riding by on the train wave to us. In fact, I think we may have become a fixture. All the ambience of a train station is a gift to the mind of a child. The questions that the children raise as a result of this exposure allow for teaching about life on many levels.

But we don't just watch. Oh no. We ride. The grandkids and I take the electric train two stops to a playground, play awhile on the slides and swings and come back home again. Once we rode for eight stops on the diesel train to another small city where we shopped for a birthday gift, and ate dinner before returning home the same way we had come. Our biggest PT adventure was as an entire family with friends. We rode the diesel north to the end of the line in San Francisco, crossed the street to another train station, rode four stops and walked to the Sausalito Ferry. Is there a sight prettier? Think of all you can teach with the sights to be seen on and around the Bay from a ferry ride to Sausalito—a thrill for people of all ages.

Another of the more interesting PT adventures occurred just recently. As a new member of an organization called the Raging Grannies, I was asked if I would help relieve a group of women demonstrating for peace in front of Speaker Pelosi's home in San Francisco. I'd like to take public transportation. I'll join you in that said Granny Ruth. And we did. So now I can use PT to teach my grandchildren about social responsibility and political action. How great is that?

by Susan Taylor

The Active Hip Grandma

chapter 6

Let's Get Physical: Keeping in Shape for all that Babysitting

Yeah, we all hate to exercise. It's boring. Nothing worse than wasting time on a treadmill in a gym with a roomful of other sweaty gossiping grandmothers. I walk the dog, or push the grandkid in a stroller. We look at butterflies and sheep and flowers and trees: such a preferred view over the jiggly butt cheeks of the gym grannies. So get out there and walk. You'll never be Twiggy, but you can bet your sweet bippy that you'll stay in okay shape, and maybe even receive that mother of all compliments: "You look pretty good . . . for a grandmother."

1. My favorite sneakers for all that walking are Saucony. (**www.saucony.com**) Even the name sounds saucy and snappy. I got the Hurricane model, and it makes walking on concrete tolerable, if not quite pleasurable. Splurge on a workout wardrobe that makes you want to get out there and move. If you're still wearing those scary old late '70s gray sweat pants that gather around the ankles, get on the Web right now and order something new. Use the gray sweats for a cleaning rag. Throw away the 1980s activewear, too, Aerobic Woman. Neon leotards and tights are so yesterday, and your body is so today. Maybe you could stitch those leotards together, stretch them out, and make yourself a nice bright hammock. Every grandmother needs a hammock.

2. If you get the wintertime blues, keep the energy going with a light box. These things really work. I just plant my Sun Touch next to the computer for thirty minutes a day, September through April, and I'm a much happier woman. No more Seasonal Affective Disorder. You can even hear me hum John Denver's "Sunshine on my Shoulders" if you listen really closely. Sunshine on my shoulders makes me happy . . . And we all know that when Grandma's happy, everybody's happy. (**www.apollolight.com**)

There are also some very cool floor lamps with which you can read and feel better on gray days. Check out **www.ott-lite.com**—they have amazing technology that helps bifocal-assisted old granny eyes see small print like it was 1979. I love this thing. They also make a Learning Light for your grandkid, so that there's no excuse for not doing well on homework. Other good ones are available from Full Spectrum Solutions— (**www.fullspectrumsolutions.com**) and from Verilux. (**www.verilux.net**)

③ Don't have Granny arms. Those wings flapping in the wind as you wave goodbye to the kid are so not attractive. Weight-bearing exercise three times a week reduces the risk of osteoporosis (broken hips and hunchbacks are not cool, Grandma), and it benefits not just the bones, but the heart, coordination, balance, and posture too. Get some hand weights and lift 'em. You won't look like Halle Berry, but it'll get you in shape for lifting the kid. The coolest new weights are Hampton's Jelly Bells, made from urethane rather than vinyl. Sleek and stylin', these dumbbells come in hot colors and look great sitting in your living room. You can find them at sporting goods stores nationwide. (**www.hamptonfit.com**) Another cool hand weight is the Aqua Bell. You fill them with water to whatever weight works, so it's fun to travel with dumbbells. And no, I'm not talking about your family. (**www.aquabells.com**)

Get in Shape with a Vibrator

The Soloflex Whole Body Vibration (WBV) Platform sends mechanical vibrations pulsing through your body, taking all the work out of exercising. It improves circulation, strength, flexibility, and balance. And it feels good too. You can stand on it, sit on it, lie down on it ... starting at just ten minutes a day. Yes, yes, yes! Meg Ryan, eat your heart out. (www.soloflex.com)

Become One (Hummmm) by Practicing Yoga with the Grandyogi

1. You can find easy (ahem!) yoga poses for kids and adults of all ages at **www.susankramer.com**. Down Dog isn't just for Cat Stevens anymore. After all, isn't grandmothering all about flexibility?! As a babysitting grandma with a way-too-busy schedule, I can personally attest to the benefits of twisting yourself into poses that you once thought were subhuman. You too can discover the Zen of diaper changing, which is much easier than motorcycle maintenance.

2. Get a Mr. Pretzel Yogi Bendo toy (and bend him into positions that you could never do) from Peaceful Company. Go to **www.peacefulcompany.com** and type "Mr. Pretzel" in the search bar.

3. Help other people's grandkids by buying a handmade bag for your yoga mat from **www.forgottenchildren.net**. Profits help to abolish child slave labor, and to feed hungry kids. I don't know about you, but my grandmother radar flashes emergency red at the thought of a child with an empty belly. We grandmothers need to unite: Feed the world!

Keep that Yoga Mat Clean

Yoga mats are on the floor. The floor is dirty. You can't center yourself when germs are in your face. Clean that mat with all-natural products from **www.stirlenchi.com**. You can find cool mats at **www.drishtiyoga.com**. I got the Sunrise style, and it makes me feel oh, so Zen-ish. I also ordered an orange Hibiscus mat from **www.wailana.com**, and the cheery pattern could almost convince you that you have been magically transported to Hawaii.

Born to Be Wild:
Grandma is a Biker Chick

One young grandmother I know rides a pink Harley, personalized with her name and painted daisies. She wears black leather and rocks out to AC/DC. Bet she's popular with the soccer moms when she roars into the school parking lot to pick up the grand-biker. If choppers, low-riders, and bikes are your passion, get the grandkid these rumbly gifts:

1. A rocking motorcycle (you know, instead of a rocking horse?). This thing rocks, literally. Go to **www.gotobaby.com** and type "rocking motorcycle" in the search bar.

2. A kick-ass little leather jacket just like Grandma's from **www.babybiker.co.uk**.

3. A Harley-Davidson-made piggy bank, so that the little one can start her own Harley fund. Go to **www.hdart.com** and click on "Biker Pottery."

Later, Skater

Skateboarding is one of the hottest sports for kids of today. Get in on the act, Gram, and the grandkid will love to tell his friends that he has a skater Granny. Check out **www.longboardlarry.net** for high-quality custom long boards made from Baltic birch. Get one for the grand-skater. Get one for yourself. Hum Beach Boys tunes. Wear knee pads, elbow pads, and a helmet. Good luck. Been nice knowing you.

Fun Ways to Exercise

1. Invented in 1919, the Pogo stick is still around and hopping. Get one for the kid, then get one for yourself. It's great exercise, and good for the old-lady circulation. They now have a frog hopper that's jumpin' for toddlers, and some extreme daredevil pogos for the Evel Teen Knievel. (**www.pogostickusa.com**)

2. Remember your old pink Hula Hoop from the 1960s? Well, girlfriend, Hula Hooping is all the rage nowadays. These hoops are heavy-duty, and so not the cheapo toys of our day. It's been proven that hooping melts belly fat, and don't we all need that? Check out **www.hoopgirl.com** for the hippest hoops in the universe. Another great site is **www.bettyhoops.com** Boop-boop-dee-hoop!

3. Straight from the UK and now on American shores is the first portable pole dancing kit. Come on, Grandma, this is a fun and non-sleazy workout that's good for the body and the libido. It's not just for skanks, although there are a lot of them in the industry. Anyway, you're not a pro, Ms. Pole. This is for exercise, in your own home, with nobody leering at you. The package comes with a pole that easily goes up and down in less than a minute (that's more than you can say about Grandpa, huh?), as well as an instructional DVD, garter belt, and fake dancer dollars. When your significant other starts to whine that all you think about is the grandkid then just whip out your pole and shut him up. (**www.peekaboousa.com**)

Green Granny:
Environmental Awareness

You recycle. You still have your old copy of Rachel Carson's "Silent Spring." Earth Day is a big holiday for you. You don't throw Diet Coke cans out your car window. You want to save the Earth for your grandkid, before it's way too late, and we're all living in global warming hell, melting like the Wicked Witch of the West. Depressed? Well, then do your part, dammit.

1. Save all of your magazines and create paper sculptures by rolling individual pages into thin tubes. Glue these together in the shape of ships or houses or trains or whatever your environmental heart desires. It sounds weird, but it looks splendidly ecologically-minded.

2. Research companies that use biodegradable containers and buy their goods. Carpool. Turn off lights when you're not in the room. Don't drive humungous Hummers or SUV's, unless you're in the Army or have six kids. Recycle your plastic and aluminum, and teach the green grandkid to do the same.

3. Read recycling books such as Barn Savers (shameless plug for my husband's business) and *The Earth and I* by Frank Asch.

Go Organic

Katharine Hamnett has reissue organic shirts that'll make your politics clear to anybody who can read. "Choose Life," "Clean Up Our Die," and "Worldwide Nuclear Ban NOW" are some of your choices in these ethically and environmentally made shirts. (www.katharinehamnett.com)

Rage Against the Machine:
Activist Grandma

The older you get, the braver you get. You're comfortable in your own skin, saggy and wrinkled though it may be. We've been through Watergate and Kent State, Tricky Dick and Vietnam, Woodstock and Patty Hearst, women's lib and civil rights, Roe vs. Wade and *Kramer vs. Kramer*. We've seen the first man walk on the moon, and we know how to reach for it. We're strong, we're tough, and we weren't born yesterday. Stand up for what you believe, girlfriend. The future is for our grandkids, and we need to fight for their rights. Rage on!

1. The Raging Grannies are an activist group based in California. Active in San Francisco and the surrounding Peninsula, the Grannies wear long skirts and funky hats, granny glasses and cool shoes. They hand out peace buttons on school campuses, and advise students as to their rights with military recruiters. (Don't even get me started on this one. An Army recruiter almost had my son, 19 at the time. Justin was ready to sign the contract on the evening of 9-10-01. "Wait a minute," I said as he put pen to paper. "What happens in the very improbable circumstance of America going to war somewhere?" The recruiter stammered and fumbled with his papers, stating that was a "clause in the contract" that he'd have to bring back later in the week. I wouldn't allow my kid to sign without that clause. My kid wasn't happy. Neither was the recruiter. Well, the next morning was 9-11, and my son decided that he did not want to sign the contract, clause or no clause. I was harassed with phone calls from the pissed-off recruiter, who called my son "wimpy" and "wuss.")

Whew. Like I said, don't get me started. If Justin had signed that contract, I have a strong feeling that I would not be a grandmother at this time, of this darling little boy of mine. And then this book wouldn't exist. So anyway, since it does exist, I'll just stop ranting and give you the Raging Grannies's Web address.: **www.raginggrannies.com**.

2 20% of the population in South Africa is dying of AIDS, leaving lots of children without parents. Grandmas are stepping up to the plate, and raising orphaned grandkids, sometimes increasing their families to the point where they're feeding between ten and twenty-five children. More than thirty grandmothers have joined forces in an outreach project called the Gogo Grannies. (Gogo is the South African word for grandmother.) Supporting one another in the struggle to feed and clothe their grandchildren, the women have bonded together with a group called Keep a Child Alive. (**www.keepachildalive.org**)

3 The Granny Peace Brigade is fighting like hell for peace. Feisty and determined, these grannies tried to enlist in the military so that their grandkids wouldn't have to. They were arrested, handcuffed, and hauled off. Didn't stop 'em. This is one spirited bunch of broads. (**www.grannypeacebrigade.org**)

Wear It to Share It

Wear your peace belief on a cool shirt from **www.besodoso.com**. Sharing the love, spreading the word, and believing in peace–this is one hip little hippie company. Olivia Newton-John agrees. She wore their "It Is What It Is" shirt on American Idol, bringing instant attention to this company whose motto is "Be the person we were so put on this earth to be, and do as we were so meant to do." Be So Do So. Good motto for any hip grandma.

Rock Out With Your Own Hip Grandmas Club Band

I've played electric guitar since I was eleven and have played in several bands throughout the years. The most fun band ever, though, has been my Hip Grandmas Club Band.

If you'd like to form a Hip Grandmas Club band, choose band members who can actually play. Lessons might be necessary. You'll need a drummer, a lead guitarist, a rhythm guitarist, a bass player, and a vocalist. The vocalist should be the best-looking grandmother, and the dumbest one can be the drummer. If you have a really stupid grandmother who wants to join, put her on a tambourine and have her sing backup.

Get guitars from Daisy Rock Girl Guitars (**www.daisyrock.com**). They're pink and purple and girly, and Daisy Rock is proud to be the official guitar of The Hip Grandmas Club. Get the grandkid his or her first guitar from **www.musicforlittlepeople.com**. I got the blue half-size acoustic for Connor, and it's the sweetest little guitar on the planet.

Write songs about your grandkids and the art of cool grandmothering. Dress hip. Dance. Watch MTV for ideas on wardrobe and dance moves. Modify slightly for your body type. Don't play anything by the Carpenters or Olivia Newton John. Covers by Pink Floyd, Led Zeppelin, Nirvana, Tom Petty, and the Grateful Dead are approved by the group, as are any of the Club songs on the list:

Let's Spend the Night Together
(with thanks to the Rolling Stones)

My, My, My, My
Don't you worry 'bout what's on your mind (Oh my)
Granny's in a hurry and I can't take my time (Oh my)
I'm going red and my tongue's getting tied (tongues's getting tied)
I'm off my head and my mouth's getting dry.
I try. I ask Mom and Dad and I try (Oh my)

Let's spend the night together
Now I need you more than ever
Let's spend the night together now
I feel so strong that I can't disguise (oh my)
Let's spend the night together
But I just can't apologize (oh no)
Let's spend the night together
Hope they don't hang me up and let me down (don't let me down)
We could have fun just groovin' around, around, and around
Oh my, my
Let's spend the night together
Now I need you more than ever
Let's spend the night together
Let's spend the night together
Grandma needs you more than ever
You know I'm smiling baby
You need some guiding baby
I'm just deciding baby now
I need you more than ever
Let's spend the night together
Let's spend the night together now
This doesn't happen to me everyday (oh my)
Let's spend the night together
No excuses offered anyway (oh my)
Let's spend the night together
I'll satisfy your every need (every need)
And I now know you will worship me
Oh my, my, my, my, my
Let's spend the night together
Now I need you more than ever
Let's spend the night together now

Don't Worry, Baby
(with thanks to the Beach Boys)

Well, it's been building up inside of me
For oh I don't know how long
I don't know why
But I keep thinking
Something's bound to go wrong

But she looks in my eyes
And makes me realize
And she says "Please get me, Grandma"
Don't worry, baby
Don't worry, baby
I'm gonna con Mom and Dad tonight

Don't worry baby
Don't worry baby
Don't worry baby

I guess I should've kept my mouth shut
When I started to brag about that girl
But I can't back down now:
I pushed the other grandmas until they hurled.

She makes me come alive
And makes me wanna lie
When she says "Don't worry Grandma"
Don't worry baby
Don't worry baby
Everything will turn out alright

Don't worry baby
Don't worry baby
Don't worry baby

She told me, "Grandma, when you call today
Just tell them something good about what we'll do.
And if you know how much I loved you, Granny,
nothing could go wrong with you."

Oh what she does to me
When she makes that call to me,
And she says don't worry Grandma.
Don't worry baby
Don't worry baby
Everything will turn out alright

Don't worry baby
Don't worry baby
Don't worry baby

Another Brick in the Wall
(with thanks to Pink Floyd)

We don't need no parents' rules.
We don't need no Mom control.
No Dad's curfews on a school night.
Parents, leave those kids alone.
Hey! Parents! Leave those kids alone!
All in all, it's just another brick in the wall.
All in all, you're just another brick in the wall.

We don't need no green veggies.
Grandma will buy you a new cell phone.
No early bedtime on a week night.
Parents, leave those kids alone.
Hey! Parents! Leave those kids alone!
All in all you're just another brick in the wall.
All in all you're just another brick in the wall.

I Want to Hold Your Hand

(with thanks to the Beatles)

Oh yeah, Kid, I'll tell you something,
I think you'll understand
When I say that something
I want to hold your hand,
I want to hold your hand,
Granny wants to hold your hand.

Oh please, say to me
You'll let me be your Gran.
And please, say to me
You'll let me hold your hand.
Now let me hold your hand,
I want to hold your hand.

And when I touch you I feel happy inside.
It's such a feeling that my love
I can't hide, I can't hide, I can't hide.

Yeah you've got that something,
I think you'll understand.
When I say that something
I want to hold your hand,
I want to hold your hand,
Granny wants to hold your hand.

And when I touch you I feel happy inside.
It's such a feeling that my love
I can't hide, I can't hide, I can't hide.

Kid, you've got that something,
I know you'll understand.
When I feel that something
I want to hold your hand,

I want to hold your hand,
I want to hold your hand,
Granny wants to hold your hand.

Every Breath You Take
(with thanks to the Police)

Every breath you take
Every move you make
Every bond you break
Every step you take
Grandma's watching you

Every single day
Every word you say
Every game you play
Every night you stay
Grandma's watching you

Oh, can't they see
You belong to ME!
How my poor heart aches
With every step you take

Every move you make
Every vow you break
Every smile you fake
Every claim you stake
Grandma's watching you

Since you went home I been lost without a trace
I dream at night I can only see your face
I look around but it's you I can't replace
I feel so cold and I long for your embrace
I keep crying baby, baby, please...

Oh, cant you see
You belong to me
How my poor heart aches
With every breath you take

Every move you make
Every vow you break
Every smile you fake
Every claim you stake
Grandma's watching you

Every move you make
Every step you take
Grandma's watching you

Consciousness, Conscience and Consequences

Last November I participated in the sixteenth annual vigil and protest at the gates of the U.S. Army base in Fort Benning, Georgia. Built on an old plantation, the huge base houses a training school for Latin American soldiers. This school, which was originally established in Panama in 1946, came to be known as the School of the Americas. Latin Americans call it School of Assassins because of the history of its graduates' murderous abuse of citizens designated as "insurgents" by the ruling powers.

This year, inspired by Holly Near's song "1,000 Grandmothers," describing the compassion, wisdom and forceful strength of grandmothers, I initiated a campaign by calling one thousand grandmothers to Fort Benning to help close this school. My conscience exhorted my grandmother soul to take a stand that would be noticed. I aimed to stand in the way of business-as-usual at Fort Benning. This involved crossing onto an army base through a hole in the fence, because the gates were locked to prevent entry by protestors. I and fifteen others were promptly arrested, handcuffed, videotaped, and tagged.

Some ask, "What is the point of being arrested? What good would it do? Why would you, a law abiding person, even think of doing something so futile, and maybe dangerous?" There really is nothing good about being arrested. The point, though, is not to be arrested: it is to resist an evil.

—*Cathy Webster*
Hip Grandma Activist
Written from the Sacramento County Jail

Make Sure that Their Divorce Doesn't Divorce You

I was divorced from my first husband. My parents are divorced from each other. I know divorce like the back of my age-spotted hand. If the parents of your grandkid decide to do the "D word," don't dwell upon the negatives. Yeah, it's a bummer, but it'll work out okay. Look at the plus side: The child will still have you as a stable force in his life. Much as they might like to, the parents can never divorce you. Every state in the U.S. now has Grandparents' Rights Laws, and that's a good thing. So stop humming those sad Barry Manilow songs, because you're annoying people.

Two words of advice: "Be available." Oh, two more: "Stay connected." Well, while I'm at it, how about two more: "No opinions." If you feel compelled to offer your viewpoint on the ex-spouse, bite your tongue. Hard. This is not the *Jerry Springer Show*. This is real life, and every kid loves his parents. Two parents. One love. Shut up.

Turning Memories into Memoir

Get your memories on paper so that the grandkid will have that even after you'e gone. Even non-writers can create a great journal keepsake for the younger ones. Call me. We'll talk. I teach a fun and productive Hip Grandmas Writing Workshop.

If You're Raising the Grandkid

If your grandchild sends his Mother's Day card to you, you're **more than a grandmother.** You're a mother of a grandmother. You're busy, you're tired, and sometimes you think you're too damn old for this gig. But you're not. You can do it, girl. Chin up. At least ten percent of American children are being raised by grandparents. You're not alone. Get real. Taking care of business isn't so bad. Put on your Superwoman cape and make your way through the days. Keep yourself healthy, because that kid needs you. If you're raising the child because of parental problems like drugs or abuse or whatever, it's a drag, but don't talk trash about the parents. If you don't have something nice to say, don't say anything at all.

Step Grandkids, Half Grandkids, Sometimes Grandkids: These Are Confusing Times

My stepson has a great baby named Jack. If you want to get technical, Jack is my step-grandson. That's a bulky term, and it sounds like an exercise device that's way too painful. If you have step-grandkids, forget the "step." They're your grandkids. If your kid marries somebody who already had a kid with somebody else, it gets a little hairy. (The relationship, not the kid.) What should this kid call you? What should you call this kid? What if you don't like the new kid as much as you love and adore your flesh and blood grandkids? Keep it a secret. Nobody needs to know. Just give it time. Even *The Brady Bunch* wasn't perfect, you know.

Hip Grandma Activities for 3 to 6 Year Old Grandkids

chapter 7

The Kid Is Past Two
(And Sometimes You Allow Him to
Stay Up that Late Too)

By now, he's starting to figure out that you're cool. You don't want to blow that image, so here is a week's worth of wacky to keep the reputation going.

Snowman Sunday

Order a gigantic inflatable snowman from www.bronners.com. Get the biggest one that you can get. Convince your spouse that it's really not embarrassing to have a snowman that's taller than your house. Blow it up. Put it in the yard. Have it there when the child arrives, and watch the surprise in his eyes. Ignore the rolled eyes of his parents. Kiss the snowman's belly, and lift the grandkid so that he can do it too. Take the kid inside, where you've hung a string of snowman lights from **www.oogalights.com.** Read books about snowmen, such as *A Snowman Named Just Bob* and *Snowmen at Night.* Shake the snow globe that you've bought just for today. Make an ice cream sundae on Snowman Sunday, or serve snowman ice cream treats that you found at Wal-Mart. You could also cut toast with circle cookie cutters, spread soft cream cheese, and decorate the snowman (or woman) with raisins, carrots, and chocolate chips. Watch a "Frosty The Snowman" DVD and sing along with the song. Unplug the inflatable giant snowman and watch it collapse into a heap. Tell the kid that the snowman is taking a nap, and that he should too. Plug it back in when he wakes up. If it's wintertime and there's real snow outside, make a real snowman. If you're holding Snowman Sunday in July, go outside in a knit hat and mittens. Pose beside the giant snowman, and wave goodbye when the child leaves with his parents. Let him take the snow globe. Tell him to bring it back for the next Snowman Sunday. Ignore the sighs of the parents. Just because they're too mature to be immature doesn't mean that you can't have some fun.

Monkey Monday

Buy a bunch of bananas. Order a Barrel of Monkeys from Amazon or Hasbro (**www.hasbro.com**). (These will bring back good childhood memories for you, and they still cost only about $3.99.) Dig out any stuffed monkeys that you may have (mine is from **www.folkmanis.com**), as well as any books about monkeys (*Curious George* and *Five Little Monkeys Jumping on the Bed* are easy to find.) Walk like a monkey and make monkey noises when the grand-monkey arrives. Dress in brown. If you have brown fur, that's even better. If you're really crafty, make a sock monkey. Buy one if you're not (**www.supersockmonkey.com**). Eat the bananas, either plain or on ice cream. Talk about how Barrel of Monkeys and sock monkeys were really popular when you were a kid. Let the grand-monkey jump on your bed. Tell him about how there was a band called The Monkees when you were a kid. Explain that they were men, not monkeys. Download clips of Monkees songs from **www.monkees.net.** Teach the grand-monkey to sing "Hey, Hey We're the Monkees!" Make the stuffed monkey sing it too. Sing it really loudly when your child arrives to pick up his child. Walk like a monkey when you go outside to wave goodbye. Ignore your child's snide comments about needing medication or a padded room.

Twister Tuesday

Buy a Twister game, or dig your old one out from the attic. Buy some licorice twists and pretzel twists and bread twists. Download the song "The Twist" by Chubby Checker. Dance "The Twist" when the child arrives. Teach her how to dance it too. Eat the food twists. Play a game of "Twister." Laugh hysterically. Play again. Dance again. Watch the beginning of "The Wizard of Oz" and talk about how twisters are tornados. Pretend that your house has landed in Oz. Draw twisty pictures together. End Twister Tuesday by spinning in circles.

Wild West Wednesday

Get a DVD of *The Lone Ranger* or *Bonanza* or whatever your childhood favorite western show might be. Order cowboy hats from **www.cowboyhatstore.com**. Decorate the house with whatever western stuff you might have on hand: ropes, saddles, vests with fringes, chaps, spurs, boots. Play your favorite country-western music. Read "Little Red Cowboy Hat" or another cowboy/wild west book. (There are zillions of them on Amazon.) Make a campfire (outside) if your city ordinance allows. If not, don't try it. Fines and jail time are not cool. Just use the microwave to make s'mores. Use theme plates from **www.partypoopers.com**. Pretend that the kid is your grand-cow, and rope him. Say YEE-HAW! Teach him to sing Kris Kristofferson songs. Rope the kid's parents when they walk in, and insist that they sit through a country-western concert recital. Give them a s'more, and ignore their grumpy comments about theme days being so lame.

Thomas Thursday

This one's a no-brainer: *Thomas The Tank Engine.* All Thomas, all the time. So easy to find the goods; so easy to pull off. Watch the DVDs. Make a Thomas cake. Use Thomas plates and cups and napkins. Take a trip to a train museum, if there's one within driving distance. Read train books. Snuggle up under a Thomas blanket. Thomas is hot, and you'll be so cool if you know about him too. The Web site **www.learningcurve.com** has lots of Thomas products, and so does every other toystore in the universe.

Furry Friday

Visit a petstore or animal shelter. Talk about fur, touch fur. Learn about animals, and talk about the pets of your past. Tell tales of your childhood dog Fido, a dog who liked to read. The grandkid will love hearing the stories of Granny as a girl (gasp!), and the furballs that she loved. Draw pictures of furry creatures. Eat something fur-like (not mold, you poor housekeeper, you).

Cotton candy works. Dig out your old fur coats, and make a crafty project out of fake fur from the art store. When the parents arrive for their child, inform them that it was "a good time, fur sure." Once again, ignore the sighs and rolled eyes. Hum Cyndi Lauper's "Girls Just Want to Have Fun" as you wave goodbye.

Silly Saturday

Use combos of ideas from other theme days, or add your own touches and ideas. Use your imagination, crazy lady. What do I have to do: create a whole dang week for you?! Lose your inhibitions and gain the power of entertaining the grandkid beyond his wildest dreams. He'll never forget you, and neither will the neighbors who've been hiding behind their curtains watching all this lunacy. You are woman: Let me hear you roar. Invent some over-the-edge theme days, and no day will be mundane. There's one word that's a curse word in the Grandma's Dictionary: boring. Shudder. So go for it. Silly Saturday is yours for the taking. Be free as a butterfly, uninhibited as a kid, weird and wacky as Gilda Radner on *Saturday Night Live*. You are the star. Shine.

More Fun Stuff

1. Bubbles never go out of style, Granny. Everybody loves 'em. Produce hundreds of bubbles without blowing by getting a Gazillion Bubbles machine at **www.funrise.com**. For $9.99, you can save yourself the trouble of forming your lips into an "O" and giving yourself even more of those crinkles around the mouth.

2. Baseball is as American as apple pie, Grandma, so be sure that you encourage the grandkid to play it. Get out there and throw with her. It'll exercise those floppy granny arms. Run bases for thunder-thigh therapy. You'll hit a home run if you give the kid his first mitt, personalized with his name and birth date, along with a customized bat and ball. The glove comes in girly pink or boy blue, and it'll be sure to be saved after serving its purpose. Dig out those peanuts and Cracker Jacks, and get crackin' on this order. **www.nokona.com**. (Click on "Children's Gifts.")

3. Old-fashioned, inexpensive fun is to be had on windy springtime days. There's a big selection of kites nowadays, so choose a couple of them and get out there with the kid. Try **www.breezechasers.com** for a selection that'll make you the wind beneath your grandkid's wings. I got the Beetle stunt kite, and it's a blast . . . for both of us. Check out the safety tips on the Web site, and stay away from those power lines.

4. Historic children's gardens are springing up all over the country, thanks to the Monticello program that encouraged schools to plant gardens commemorating Thomas Jefferson's 250th birthday. Cleverly put together by the Monticello Education Center and the Thomas Jefferson Center for Historic Plants, the Monticello Children's Garden Kit includes easy-to-grow plants. (**www.monticello.org**)

Ho, Ho, Ho

Ho, ho, ho. That means Christmas, not a trio of prostitutes. A time of stress, suicide, and dysfunctional families forced to act happy, Christmastime has become commercialized to the point of crassness. Try not to let the pimped-out whoring of a holy holiday harsh your mellow. Do some incredible stuff that doesn't require trying to park at the mall or eating with people you don't like. If you're Jewish or Jehovah's Witness or agnostic or atheist, you can still have grandmotherly fun with America's number one crazy-maker. Ho, ho, ho.

❶ Get a Light Flurries machine, and fake the neighbors out with false snow. A revolutionary outdoor lighting system that creates the illusion of flurries, this thing sets up in 5 easy minutes and gives you and the grandkids hours of pleasure. Google "light flurries machine."

❷ Snuggle on the sofa and read some Christmas books to the grand reader. Some of the most beautifully written and illustrated are *The Most Precious Gift* by Marty Crisp, The *Last Chimney of Christmas Eve* by Linda Oatman High (yeah, that's me; what did you think, that I could make a living by writing only books about cool grandmothers?), and *The Mouse Before Christmas* by Michael Garland. For mood-inducing background music, play Vince Guaraldi's "A Charlie Brown Christmas."

❸ Start a Christmas tradition with Elf On The Shelf. We had one of these when I was a kid, and I've relived the memories by ordering one from **www.elfontheshelf.com**. Every time the grandkid comes to visit, the elf should be in a different spot, as this busy little elf frequently leaves to report children's behavior to the North Pole. Nice will win out over naughty when the elf is on your shelf.

Keep It Even

To avoid the "my kid got less than his" syndrome, keep it even in the gift-giving department. Grandmothers of more than one can establish a pattern for birthdays and holidays, and just get the same thing for each grandkid. As someone who raised stepkids, I've become an old pro at this. Even in the all-your-own-flesh-and-blood families, those annoying little spats can arise. Grandmas naturally become more attached to the kid that they see the most. If you're a Granny Nanny who's giving a lot of help in the childcare department, you're bonded at the hip to that kid. Connor's part of our family at least three days a week; we see Jack maybe once a month. Here's our birthday pattern so far:

First birthday: Power Wheels L'il Quad riding toy. Less than a hundred bucks at Wal-Mart, Toys 'R Us, and a million other places.

Birthday Number Two: Remote controlled airplane. Fun for The Dad and The Kid, and easy to find on the web and in stores.

Third Birthday: Musical instrument. A real one. A good resource is **www.musicforlittlepeople.com**

Mirror, mirror on the wall; who's the fairest one of all? You are, my fair lady. Life's not fair. . . but you can be, so keep it even.

Some of my best memories *of childhood Christmases revolve around watching the old TV specials: "Rudolph The Red-Nosed Reindeer", "Frosty The Snowman", "Santa Claus is Coming To Town." All written by Romeo Muller, these original Christmas classics have been collected into a great boxed set available at online and brick and mortar stores. Titled "The Original Television Christmas Classics," this collection is a must-have for Grandma's house. And nowadays, the kids don't have to wait another year to watch it again: They can play these over and over, until dreams—or nightmares —of Burl Ives dance through Granny's mind.*

Rebirth

Many many years ago, when my husband and I were newly married, we dreamed and hoped our life would be filled with happiness and love of children. Our first born, a son, was a joy. He ate, he slept, and he smiled all the time.

Wow, this is easy. We could have a dozen. A few years later, we had a daughter—also a joy. She ate, she smiled and she never slept. Maybe this was a message. We went to science fairs, soccer games, field trips, vacations, worked at the schools—wow, this is fun. Every night we would tuck the tots into bed, and we would whisper in their ears: "Don't grow up to be a cowboy" to our son, and to our daughter, "Never go west of the Mississippi."

The years passed and the children grew up and they went to college (on the East Coast of course). And then they soared with new wings to new stages in their lives:

Our son: "I'm going to study Physics in Santa Barbara. I will just be there for a short time ... and it is only a three-hour time change. I'll be back!!!"

Our daughter: "Mom and Dad, my husband (did I forget to say our baby got married?) and I are just going out to San Francisco for a couple of years. We will be back! And it is only a three-hour time change."

So both of our babies were out west, and we were always looking at our watches. Two exciting things happened last year: Our fist born got married and moved back to the East Coast, and I at 60 became a mom again ... that's right. I had a baby—sort of.

My labor was five hours on the plane, and when I got to the hospital, I was handed a beautiful baby girl. You have all this love for the baby you hold, and it was like giving birth with no pain. You love this as if it is yours—and it is—so I did give birth at 60! It is hard to explain how you feel when your baby has a baby, but it is the most special moment in your life.

Now I'm a hip grandma (or "Mema" as I hope to be called).

I feed my granddaughter, we play with toys, we walk in the park (when my husband and I are out west), and we play on our computer. We chat on line and we can blow kisses and give hugs as we video chat (a must to learn if you haven't). We love to watch her face light up as she sees us and we see her. We can play peek-a-boo, we can hear and watch her whistle, wave, "play how big". So I know it is hard to believe, and I should be some medical wonder; but I gave birth again—and this is the best stage of life ... that's way it's called GRAND!

—*Inez Grimaldi*
Hip Grandma
Potomac, Maryland

Hip Grandma Activities
for Grandkids Ages 6 to 12

chapter 8

Grandma Outside

Helping to teach your grandkid to pedal a bike is such a sweet pleasure. It's an old-fashioned out-in-the-fresh-air activity that'll get the young one into the great outdoors for a change. The wind in your hair, sunshine on your shoulders, blue sky above, green grass below . . . Ahhhh. It's like a John Denver song. It makes you high. It makes you happy. Bike on!

1 The coolest tricycle that I've ever seen is the City Trike. I got one for Connor, and he's the most stylin' trike-rider in this one-horse town. Bright primary colors and sturdy steel construction make this a supreme first bike. It's sleek, contemporary, and rugged, all at once. I wish there was one in my size. Made in Italy by Italtrike (**www.italtrike.com**), you can order the bike from Sparkability. Click on "Ride On Toys" at **www.sparkability.com**.

2 You're a classic, right? So get yourself a classic Nirve cruiser bike from California, baby. I've got my eye on the plumeria 3-speed Island Flower cruiser: Pink. With painted flowers. White sidewalls. Are you salivating yet? Just because you're now a grandmother doesn't mean that you can't still be a girly-girl. (**www.nirve.com**)

3 Buy the kid a good helmet because his genius brain is worth protecting. (Your brain's already shot, honey, so it's not quite as important for your head.)

Sandbox Safety

Remember the no-lids sandboxes we had for our kids? Those things are disgusting, and it's amazing that our children didn't get some cat disease. If you have a sandbox in the yard, make sure it's covered so that the neighborhood cats don't think that they have a huge litter box in your backyard. A cool sandbox is the boat-shaped one from KidKraft. (**www.KidKraft.com**)

Quirky Cookouts
to Lure Them to Your House

Hot dogs and burgers on the grill might not cut it. Maybe you need to make the cookout a clambake or a lobster boil. Some people have discriminating tastes nowadays. Whether it be Memorial Day, Independence Day, or Labor Day, invite the Grand One and his parents to a stellar cookout they'll never forget.

1. Put forest faces on any trees you may have in your yard. If you don't have trees, just nail one to the side of a building. Reminiscent of the tree faces in the *Wizard of Oz,* these are sure to fascinate and entertain. Type "Forest Faces" in the search bar on the Yardiac website, **www.yardiac.com**.

2. Get a Butter Boy from **www.wrapables.com**—to dispense fresh butter onto sweet corn. Hold those slippery cobs of corn with clever dog holders (corn dogs; get it?) from **www.theparagon.com**.

3. When the sun goes down, play Frisbee with cool light up discs from **www.niteize.com**. Psychedelic colors glow in the night as the disc floats through the darkness and right into your expert, waiting hands. Impress the whole family and tell them that you were the Frisbee Champion of Whatever County in April of 1972. In your dreams.

Slip Slidin' Away

Cool inflatable slides now come in wet/dry models. Easy to clean and so much fun, these awesome slides are safe, as long as you supervise and enforce the one-at-a-time rule. If you get a Slip N Slide, it's for the kid. You probably should not slide, as loads of accidents have happened in which older people (ahem) have jammed necks or spines upon the impact at the end. A grandmother in a neck brace is so not cool.

A Tree is the Place to Be

Be the hippest grandma in the universe by having a treehouse in the backyard. Build one yourself (or get the Hip Grandpa or Significant Other to do it), or you can order the coolest treehouse in the world from **www.danielswoodland.com**. These things are amazing, girlfriend. They come with their own tree, for God's sake: a hollowed-out California tree saved from a landfill by the sweet dudes at Daniels Woodland. Don't expect cheap. These things might require a loan, but they're guaranteed for like fifteen years. They'll get you right up to the time that your grandkid needs some time alone to, uh, read.

For the Halibut

Fishing isn't just for guys anymore, Grandma. Get yourself (or your granddaughter) a girly-girl pink rod and reel at **www.fishergirl.com**. Choose the Foxy or the Mermaid; they're both ultra-cool. Breaking boundaries and bringing females into the fishing world, Fishergirl is also socially conscious: They support finding a cure for breast cancer. And—oh my cod!? they even have a Minnow pole for the tiny fisher girl. If you have a grandson who isn't into pink mermaids, get him the manly-man Sponge Bob Floating Combo from Zebco (**www.zebco.com**). If the kid drops this in the water, it floats. If the kid drops in the water, remind him that a fishing pole may be used like a tow to pull him out. It's not a bad idea to put the kid in a lifejacket. Finis Inc. makes a nice one that'll keep your precious cargo afloat.

Highlights For Children
(and For You and the Dog Too)

Remember getting *Highlights for Children* magazine in your mailbox? No?! Whoa! What were you: deprived?! Well, at least you got to rip it off from the doctor's or dentist's office, right? It's still around today, published by the same family in the same homey place in Pennsylvania, and it still includes my fave dudes Goofus and Gallant. There are the Timbertoes and Hidden Pictures too. Awwwww. What it was, what it is, what it will be. The old-school nostalgia alone is worth the subscription.

1 **www.highlights.com**: Subscribe. Now. You know you want to.

2 When the first issue of *Highlights* arrives (in your mailbox, of course; The grandkid can read it when he gets there), celebrate by springing to have your hair highlighted. If you're really brave, go for purple or blue or green or pink streaks. The grandchild will be enchanted, and you can pretend that you love it too. Hopefully, the color will still be there for Grandparents Day at the kid's school.

3 Extend the highlights theme to the family pet, and add some orange, gold, copper, blue, or pink to the dog's fur with this ridiculously insane new product called Color Highlights from Pet Society. Safe and temporary (thank God, because who'd want a permanently pink-streaked poodle?), the beauty-for-bitches bottles may be ordered on **www.petsociety.net**. Click on "Products" and then on "Pet Beauty Line."

There's No Business Like Show Business

Give the kid some culture by taking him to the theatre and kiddie shows. Some parents think the tickets are a bit pricey, but you're the grandma. Treat him! *Sesame Street Live* is great, as is *Disney on Ice*. We took Connor to see *Monsters Inc.* and *100 Years of Magic*, and it's all he talks about.

Disgusting and Fun Recipes Using a Litterbox, Dirt, Worms, and Granny's Hand

Every grandkid associates certain foods with Grandma. Gone are the days of pink lint-covered peppermints hidden in Granny's housedress pockets. My own Grammy made hot mint tea and chocolate cocoa cake. My Nana, still living at 91, makes zucchini bread and pumpkin pie. I make Dirt and Worms. (My Easy Bake oven taught me nothing.) No matter if you're the anti-Martha Stewart of your neighborhood; these are recipes any non-domestic can make, with a little help from the kids. The following three recipes are guaranteed to thrill and totally gross out the grandkids.

Granny's Litterbox Cake

Ingredients:

1 chocolate cake mix

1 white cake mix

1 package white sandwich cookies

1 small package vanilla instant pudding mix

Green food coloring

12 small Tootsie Rolls

1 new cat litter box

1 new cat litter box liner

1 new litter sifter

Prepare cake mixes and bake according to directions. After the two cakes are cool, crumble them into a large bowl. Prepare pudding mix. Chill. Crumble the sandwich cookies. Set aside all but 1/4 cup of the crumbs. Add a few drops of green food coloring to the 1/4 cup of cookie crumbs. Mix until the food coloring is evenly distributed. Toss the cake crumbs with half of the white cookie crumbs. Add enough of the chilled pudding to moisten the mixture. Place a new liner in the new cat box. Distribute the cake mixture evenly in the litter box. Put 3 unwrapped Tootsie Rolls in a microwave-safe dish. Heat them until soft and pliable, about 10 to 20 seconds. Using your fingers, shape the ends so that they are tapered and slightly curved at the ends.

Repeat with 3 more Tootsie Rolls. Bury the Tootsie Rolls in the cake mixture. Sprinkle most of the remaining white cookie crumbs over the mixture, then scatter the green crumbs over the top. Heat the remaining Tootsie Rolls, 3 at a time, until almost melted. Scrape them off on top of the cake and sprinkle with cookie crumbs. You may also wish to artistically drape one or more Tootsie Rolls over the side of the box, sprinkling it lightly with cookie crumbs. Place the box on a newspaper. Serve with a new litter sifter. It's very important that you don't forget the word "new".

Dirt and Worms: Grandma's Flower Pot

20 ounces crushed Oreo cookies

12 ounces Cool Whip

8 ounces cream cheese

4 ounce box vanilla pudding

3 1/2 cups milk

1 cup powdered sugar

1/4 cup butter or margarine

Set aside cream butter, cream cheese, and sugar, all together. Mix pudding and milk together and then add cool whip (use large bowl). Add cream cheese, mix. Fill in a flower pot, starting with pudding mixture, cookie crumbs, worms. End with cookie crumbs so it looks like dirt in the pot. Refrigerate 1 or 2 hours. Insert some plastic flowers, if desired, so it looks like the flowers are growing in the pot. Top off with gummi worms.

Granny's Hand Punch

2 jars of Tropicana Twister (any flavor)

1 liter ginger ale

To make a frozen hand, wash a disposable glove, fill with water, seal with a rubber band and freeze until hard. Combine ginger ale and Twister juices in a punch bowl or a clean hospital bowl. Dip the frozen hand briefly in warm water, then peel off the glove. Float the prepared hand in the bowl. Add some Pop Rocks for a ghostly sizzle. Wear a really long sleeve that covers your hand, and tell the kids that you lost it making their punch. Save money for their therapy bills.

Because I Pez So

Pez candy dispensers are still around! I have jars of them from the 1980s, and now I can start collecting again. Kids love these things, because we all know there's nothing like taking candy from the mouth of Bart Simpson or Snoopy. Keep at least a dozen Pez dispensers in the kitchen drawer, especially if the grandkid's parents abide by the No Junk Food rule at their house. In this crazy world, a few candy squares aren't going to hurt anybody, right? You'll pay the dentist bill, if the parents insist.

Getting the Kid Ready for School

Get ready, Grandma. The kid is going to school. This means that, for quite possibly the first time, the child may curse. He may demand Old Navy shirts and Gap jeans. She may insist upon the evil little-girl thong panties that all her slutty little friends are wearing. You don't want to give in to stuff like this, but you want to make sure the kid is ready to learn. You also want to ensure that she's not a dork.

1. Even if the parents won't buy brand-new school clothes, you—the Hip Grandma—should. At least an outfit or two to make the kid feel really hip and trendy and blendy with the crowd. Yes, I know, you outfitted your kids from K-Mart and the Goodwill, but this is so not 1983. Add some cool stuff to the kid's wardrobe. I'm thinking that maybe some clothing designers out there want to start a line called The Hip Grandmas Club? Who'd like to help design? ME! Hello?

2. Instead of sending cupcakes for the entire class, splurge for an author visit instead. If you can't think of any authors, check the byline of this book.

3. Have a sleepover celebration on the last weekend before the first day of school. Make s'mores, organize pencils and crayons, talk about the excitement of the first day of kindergarten. Cherish these moments, because he'll be a sixth-grader before you know it.

RECESS BOO BOOs

My grandson started kindergarten this week. It's always tough when a distant dream becomes a frightening reality. The adjustment has been difficult. The first day was long and filled with anxiety. There was great apprehension, much fear and worrying, and a whole lot of sobbing . . . but I survived. The second day was a little easier for me; but my son, who is a stay-at-home dad, was a nervous wreck.

We hate to see our little sweetie grow up and go out into the big, bad world. Why do kids begin school at such a tender age, anyway? Five is so young. They should wait until at least twelve. I see these little cherubs walking to school and I wonder, "How can their mothers let them outside alone?"

I'm a little overprotective, I guess. I don't understand why Grandma can't ride the bus with him and sit next to him in school, for the first month at least. No one can protect my sweet potato like his she-bear grammie. Who will kiss his boo-boos if he falls down? Who will yell at the naughty kids who teach him bad words? Who will threaten the bullies who pick on him? Who will see that the teacher gives him the extra special attention that he deserves?

That first day, my imagination was enough to fuel my worries, but then I learned that Cobi had been beat up during recess! This is one of the worst things a grandmother can hear. (I had hoped that my biggest shock the first week of school would be hearing that he'd called the teacher a doo-doo head or a stinky face.) I should have had the foresight to pay off the playground monitor so she'd watch out for him.

It seems that my brave little man tried to rescue a first grade girl who was being harassed by an older boy. When Cobi defended her, the bigger boy knocked him down and gave him a bloody nose. Of course, Grandma wanted to go to school and give that bully what-for, visit his parents, and call the principal; but my grandson assured me that it wasn't a big deal. In fact, he seemed unbothered by the entire incident.

When I asked what happened after the boy punched him, Cobi casually explained that he hadn't hit back because he "didn't want to hurt the big kid." Grandma couldn't help but smile at that.

If you're a parent or grandparent, you probably feel as I do . . . it's harder to deal with adversities affecting our kids than it is facing things that hurt us personally. Don't you wish we could just wrap them in bubble wrap to protect them when they're away from us?

Cobi is speeding toward adulthood faster than a computer virus spreads across the Web. He recently took the training wheels off his bike. He's growing up! Before I know it, he'll be driving the car, having children of his own, and visiting me in the old fogies' home. (At least I hope he'll visit.)

I hope that time won't come too soon. There are too many fun things we need to do together before that happens. I plan to savor every one of them.

—Marsha Jordan
Hip Grandma

Hip Grandma Activities
for Teenage Grandkids

chapter 9

Pimples and Armpit Hair

When your darling grandbaby grows into a snarling teen, you may be his refuge for those times when he hates the world. Despite the acne, the sullen moods, the grody armpit hair (yikes!), he's still your baby, and you can still spoil him. In return, he might even tell you some hardcore stuff that he wouldn't want his parents to know. Here's some freakin' awesome stuff to have at your house for when the hormonally challenged young adult comes to visit.

1. Nothing says "chill out" like a tie-dye bean bag chair. It'll give you flashbacks to watching "Welcome Back Kotter" and fantasizing about that fox John Travolta. You might as well get one for each of you, because otherwise you'd be fighting for the most comfy seat in the house. (**www.thebeanbagchairoutlet.com**)

2. A light-up Christmas tree with the characters from the *Simpsons*. Doh. A no-brainer for appropriate decoration any random time of the year.

3. An antique pinball machine will make his eyes shine. You can find them online or in antique shops everywhere. *Charlie's Angels* is a cool one, as it gives you an excuse to fill the kid in on how your hair feathered like Farrah's, back in the day. Blacklight posters add to the ambience and nostalgia. I promise by the glow of blacklight and the dinging of pinballs, you'll have the coolest crib in town.

If the grandkid is struggling with acne, *take a tip from Jessica Simpson and get him some ProActive. Nothing like pimples to lower self-esteem. You should know, Grandma. Aren't you the one with menopausal acne?*

Tech Stuff for the GrandTeen

So you're a bit impaired when it comes to technology, but the grand-teen isn't. Make sure you have tech essentials at your house, and you'll be Number One in his ebook. It's a bad scene to go to grandma's house if it's like grandma's house of the 1960s. Sucks to be you if you aren't up with the new stuff. Get with it. Don't be such a spaz. The times, they are a-changing, and this isn't *Room 222*. Here are tech goods that are hot now, at this moment. May the force be with you on your tech trek.

1. Creative Zen mp3 player: He can watch movies, listen to music, and download songs from the Internet. If you're really nice, maybe he'll teach you how to use it. (**www.creative.com**)

2. Coby swiveling DVD player: So you both can watch the movie without cuddling too closely. (**www.cobyusa.com**)

3. Exilim digital camera: To capture those way-too-elusive smiles. There's an underwater version too, so you can snorkel with the grandkid and take pictures, proving how cool and adventurous you are to all of your grandmother friends. (**www.exilim.casio.com**)

You Might as Well Face It, He's Addicted to Xbox

If the grandkid is glued to the video games and seems to have absolutely no incentive for setting goals or thinking about his future career, stop the slacking by signing him up for the coolest computer camp in America: Emagination. Held in several locations across the states, this is a university for teen tech addicts, with classes in video game design and the like. (www.computercamps.com)

Oh, the Places You'll Go: the Grandkid (Finally) Graduates from High School

She's made it. Sheesh. The grandkid is out of high school, and ready to leap into the world of work or college. (Hopefully not marriage. She's way too young. Do your damndest to convince her of this.) The Graduate has a lot ahead of her. Here's to you, Mrs. Robinson. Jesus loves you more than you will know. And so does your grandkid.

Celebrate the fact that your grandchild was not left behind. She passed her tests, and now she's out. I told you those DVDs wouldn't make her stupid. Celebrate good times; come on!

1. Ciao, Baby! The best graduation trip imaginable (with you, of course) is a far-out trip to Italy. Tuscany to be exact. Cortona, to be even more exact. This is the site of the movie and book "Under the Tuscan Sun." A company called Toscana Americana offers enrichment vacation packages that are absolutely beyond belief. Prices include lodging in a one thousand-year-old monastery, tours, museums, workshops, all meals (pasta, fresh bread with olive oil, gelato; Mama Mia). When you go on the Web site, search for "Linda Oatman High" and you'll find my writing workshop. Also available are classes in jewelry-making, cooking, painting, photography, and tons more. Discounts available for groups of two (that would be you and the kid!) or more. (**www.toscanaamericana.com**)

2. Party like it's 1999 with a theme jamboree. Rent a place or have it in your backyard. Don't embarrass the kid by smooching all over him in front of his friends. Keep your lovey-dovey face on the down-low. Get your supplies from **www.shindigz.com**. The flying mortar boards banner is unique, and maybe you could replicate that with a toss of the hats by all of the grads. Mary Tyler Moore, eat your heart out!

③ Send the kid on an amazing trip with **www.travelforteens.com**. With cultural immersion trips from a dazzling array of choices—Ireland, Greece, Australia, Scotland, Spain, and lots more—this company is totally fostering global peace and understanding with itineraries that create travelers, not tourists. Going for the road least traveled, the teens get to the real heart of the culture they're exploring. Designed for teens ages 13 to18 (be careful that your graduate isn't too old), this program sends home to you an international traveler.

Grand Quotes

"A house needs a grandma in it."

~Louisa May Alcott

"Grandmothers are just antique little girls."

~Author Unknown

"If your baby is beautiful and perfect, never cries or fusses, sleeps on schedule and burps on demand, an angel all the time, you're the Grandma!"

~Teresa Bloomingdale

"Just when I thought I was too old to fall in love again, I became a Grandparent."

~Author Unknown

"Have children while your parents are still young enough to take care of them."

~Rita Rudner

Cruising
(No, This Does Not Involve Tom Cruise)

1 Most of the major cruise lines have great teenage stuff. Kids like the freedom; grandmothers need the break. Everybody's happy. Two of the best are Norweigan Cruise Lines and Crystal Cruises. Cruises are hip and hot these days: not just for grannies anymore. You don't have to play shuffleboard, or dance the tango, or be a Bingo fanatic. Just do it. Go. Sail on, wild woman.

2 For the younger set, Disney Cruise sets the standard. Nobody does it like Disney, apparently, and the kids won't be wishing upon a star for a new grandma, as long as you spring for this one. (**www.disneycruise.com**)

3 The Hip Grandmas Club Cruises are especially created for you and the grandkids. Okay; maybe we'll allow the parents too, as long as they know how to loosen up and have some fun. Keep checking our Web site for cruise details. Don't be a loser: Cruise with other members of the HGC for a vacation that'll rock your granny socks.

Sail Caribbean

Since 1979, the Sail Caribbean company has been the leader in teen sailing, scuba, and community service. Their adventures are perfect for any kid interested in marine biology, or not. With the Caribbean breeze in their hair and bright sunshine in their eyes, these kids have it made: living on a luxury catamaran, sailing, scuba diving, hiking, dancing the island fire dance in some beautiful paradise. Wow. Why didn't they have stuff like this when we were teens?! Oh, I know. Our parents and grandparents would have been too stingy to spring for it. But not you. Go for it, girlfriend. (**www.sailcaribbean.com**)

Splash: Girly Trips to the Water

If you have a granddaughter, the girly trips must be made.
Pretend you're *Thelma and Louise*, and try to pick up Brad Pitt.
(In your dreams.) Be wild; be crazy; be silly; be giddy. Take some
great jammies for the all-night talks. Chocolate to eat. Here are
three great girly getaways that all involve water.

1 Sunset Suzy's Surf Camps for Women. Suzy is a pro surfer
girl who was in the movie "Blue Crush." Held in Oahu,
Sunset Suzy's offers a package that includes beachfront
lodging, meals, and surf lessons for all ages. Nothing better
than a surfin' grandma chick on a surfboard, man. It's
totally rad. (**www.sunsetsuzy.com**)

2 Swimming with dolphins off the coast of Tortola, one of the
British Virgin Islands. This is mystical, magical, life-
changing, healing, and better than any boyfriend out there.
Remember *Flipper*? His relatives are ready to swim with you.
(**www.dolphindiscovery.com**) And if you're looking for a
luscious place to stay, check out Absolute Paradise Villas on
Pineapple Beach in St. Thomas, where the soundtrack in
your head with be a laid-back loop of Jimmy Buffet songs.
(**www.absoluteparadisevillas.com**)

3 The mermaids at Weeki Wachee Springs in Florida. What
girl doesn't love mermaids?! I saw this as a kid, and it's
STILL up and running, even in the corporate shadow of
Disney World. And here's the superb part: Some of the
mermaids in the reunion show are grandmothers. Right on.
(**www.weekiwachee.com**)

Stock up on chocolates for the girly trip. Every girl loves
chocolate, especially if you time it right. One of the best places to
score great chocolate is **www.lakechamplainchocolates.com.**
Three words: Yum. Yum. Yum.

If Your Grandkid is Hollywood-Bound

If your grandkid is Hollywood-bound and determined to make it as an actor, help him to follow his dreams. You know you wanted to be *Gidget* when you were a kid. Admit it. Live vicariously through the kid. Take it to the max, and you'll get your payback by seeing the kid on *Entertainment Tonight*. Dream on. The kid doesn't have to work for the Man, despite what his parents may think.

1 Send her to a one-week intensive acting/filmmaking workshop at the New York Film Academy. They've also got an ace one-year program, for those with lots of bread to spend on dreams. (**www.nyfa.com**)

While the grandkid's in film school, you can go shopping, touring, museum-hopping, or restaurant-scooping in the Big Apple. Check out **www.lets-do-newyorkcity.com**. They've got awesome limousine tours of the city, and wouldn't you be the hit of the film school crowd if your grandkid was picked up after class in a limo?! You brown-noser, you.

2 Stay in Manhattan with the grand-actor, spending the week at the half-hotel, half-hostel Gershwin Hotel (**www.gershwinhostel.com**). Other cool hotels are The Muse (**www.themusehotel.com**), the Library (**www.libraryhotel.com**), and the Hotel Giraffe (**www.hotelgiraffe.com**).

3 Eat at some of the fun kid-friendly theme restaurants: Mars 2112 (**www.mars2112.com**); the Jekyll & Hyde Pub (**www.jekyllpub.com**), and Ellen's Stardust Diner (**www.ellensstardustdiner.com**).

When that Baby Goes off to College

Help him to spread his wings and fly. Be proud. You've been the wind beneath his wings . . . kinda-sorta. So cry a little bit. You deserve it. Don't let him see you. Grandmas look really terrible when they cry. Just spoil that outta sight kid a bit more by getting a few special things for her dorm room:

1 A humongous honkin' tub of popcorn to ensure that the kid isn't malnourished. (**www.thepopcornfactory.com**)

2 A care package of bath soap, deodorant, toilet paper, cleaning products. Nothing worse than a dirty grandkid in a dorm room with somebody else's dirty grandkid. Ewww. (Think *Animal House*.) Oh, and if you're like super-liberal, you could throw in some condoms as well. Nothing worse than a knocked-up grandkid who became preggers because she was in a dorm room with somebody else's skank of a grandkid. Shudder. If the college-age grandkid confides secretive stuff to you, don't rag on her or narc her out to the parents. She'll never tell you anything again.

3 What students really want: Money. Money. And more money. Just make sure they hide the moolah so that they don't get ripped off.

3 Things Not to Say in front of the New College Roommate:

"Be sure that you move your bowels on a regular basis, dear."

"Oh, you should have seen how adorable he looked laying naked on that little sheepskin rug! And he still has the rug! Here it is: I brought it so that he can use it in the room! Isn't that cute?!"

"Get your sleep, sweetheart. Be careful walking alone in the dark. Call me if you need anything. Watch out for the freshman fifteen. You know you have a tendency to get a little chubby. Show up for all your classes; they're so expensive, you know. Gosh, I'm going to miss you! Call me, please. Okay? 'K?"

The Hip Grandmas Club

chapter 10

Congratulations:
You're a Lifetime (and After)
Member of The Hip Grandmas Club!

You've made it through birth and bottles, baby showers and breastfeeding disappointments, pacifiers, pack-and-plays, and the endless pee-pee and poo-poo of potty training. You've been there through the teenage mood swings and the temper tantrums and the terrible twos. You've made great memories, and managed to remain cool through eighteen more years of age added onto your face. (Have you managed to save enough for Botox, after buying the kid all that stuff?)

There's been magic and play and vacation and work, joy and tears and frustrations and fears. You can kick back and relax now, because the bond is forged. Remember how we all signed yearbooks with AFA: A Friend Always? That's you to the kid: AFA. You've put your signature on his life. You've signed her heart. The tie will never be broken, even though one day you'll be gone. (Face it, girly, it's gonna happen whether you say it out loud or not.) That's when your grandchild will be telling his grandchildren stories of the things you used to do. He'll do some of them too. The traditions live on. I know; it's poignant. Shades of Ali MacGraw in *Love Story*. (Sniff. Wipe your eyes. Watch your mascara.)

In the end, being a Member of The Hip Grandmas Club is not really about the stuff, although that was a lot of fun. It's about the love. There's always the love. The Beatles were right: All ya need is love. Ta-da-da-da-da. All ya need is love. Ta-da-da-da-da. All ya need is love, love . . . love is all ya need.

Don't worry, the love's still there, even though the grandkid may be off partying at her parents' expense. Don't watch "Girls Gone Wild," and you'll be fine. And just think: one day that grandkid may have a baby of her own . . . And TA-DA!!

Welcome to The Hip Great-Grandmas Club . . .

Peace Out.

The Rules for Forming Your Own Local Branch of The Hip Grandmas Club

1. Choose a few grandmothers. They must be cool, 24/7. No posers. This is the #1 Rule, if you noticed, so make sure that you follow it.

2. Choose a happening place to meet, like maybe a coffee shop or a bookstore (where you'll prominently display your copies of this book). Do not dress dorky for the meetings. This is very important. You may wear tiaras or HGC hats, low-rider jeans (no thongs, please, as these make you look like a sleaze-bag and that's not what we're all about), boas, leather jackets (no pleather), hot tops that show off your cleavage, and little belly shirts only if you have naval jewelry and fewer than three belly rolls. Shoes may not be grandma shoes: no Easy Stride walkers or Birkenstocks. Wear your Hip Grandmas Club temporary tattoos.

3. Laugh loudly at meetings, so that others will see that it's fun. Recruit new grandmothers who may be feeling lonely and left out of the cool group. Be chill. Eat and drink good stuff. Do not mention calories or fat or cholesterol or Jessica Simpson's hot pants. If there are random hecklers (such as those in the traditional grandmother group who may attempt to hurl insults such as "immature" or "silly"), ignore the first two attempts at degradation, but then you may feel free to give the hecklers the finger. Just one. The double finger is reserved for those times when the grandkid's parents are being extra-annoying.

4. Every other month, bring the grandkid to a designated meeting. Have fun, together, Hip Grandmas and Kids. The Parents of the Kids are so not invited. Turn off your cell phones so that the Parents don't keep calling. Ignore their curfews, and pretend that your watch was broken.

⑤ Once a year, take a trip with your branch of The Hip Grandmas Club. Do not invite husbands or boyfriends. To qualify as a "trip," the journey must be at least two hours by motorcycle, car, train, or plane. Do not hitchhike. Yes, I know it was safe back in the '70s, but this is so not cool nowadays. It's not okay. Yeah, I know you're too old and unattractive to be raped, but people still might kill you.

The Vow

I, _____ (insert your grandmother name), promise to love, comfort, honor, cherish and protect my grandchild(ren) _____ in sickness and in health, through sleepless nights and crazy days, in good times and in bad, for better or worse, through good grades and through Fs, for as long as we both shall live.

Appendices, Web Sites, and Resources

A Grandmother's Non-Complicated Guide to the Worldwide Web

I'll make this very short, and easy enough for any non-techno to master. Keep it simple, and you'll be the Empress of the Web in no time.

1 Get a computer. Turn it on. Hook up to the Internet. If you don't know how to do this first step, grab a grandkid.

2 Choose a search engine. This is much easier than choosing a car engine. I like Google. Type **www.google.com** into the address bar, and TA-DA! Google at your service. There are a zillion others from which to choose, too, including Yahoo, HotBot, Alta Vista, Lycos. Take your pick.

3 If you're searching for something, just type those terms into the search bar. Say you want a swimming pool. Type in "swimming pool" or "pool" or "swimming pool for children" or "pool above-ground." You can try combining words in varied orders for different results.

4 After you type your term into the search bar and enter/click, lots of options will appear. Click on any that don't seem to be porn. Well, um, unless you want porn, of course.

5 Once you're on a Website, it's pretty self-explanatory. Shopping is easy on the Web; much simpler than schlepping around the mall. Most e-commerce sites have their own little search bars (where you can type in what you are looking for), and also sections where merchandise is divided according to type. Click on them as needed.

6 Some people are paranoid about using their credit cards online. There's no need to be nervous if you're using a reputable site.

Learn how to use the address bar, too. It's the thing at the top of the page: white, narrow, hand-length. Type in **www.eons.com**, and check out a site that's just for Boomers like you, you Web-savvy Boomer, you. **www.thenostalgicboomer.com** is another. Oh, and don't forget **www.hipgrandma.com**.

You see: It's easy, Ms. Savvy-On-The-Internet! Investigate, play, search, and don't be afraid to mess up the computer. You can't do it, even if you try. There are always computer gurus who can fix things. One thing to be wary of, though, are any emails that may arrive asking for you to click on links and give your personal information. Don't do it. Just Say No.

The Worldwide Web can connect you with old friends. You can research your family roots, plan a reunion, find the lyrics to any old song you can imagine, discover recipes, or make a hotel reservation. You can spy on your grandkid's My Space site, or make your own.

Now go to it. Geek on, grandma.

Toys

www.itoyboxes.com - First step is to get a toy box in which to keep all the stuff.

www.imagiPlay.com - Environmentally friendly toy company run by a grandmother!

www.alextoys.com - Artsy toys.

www.tinylove.com - Soft developmental toys.

www.FatBrainToys.com - To expand your grand-genius's brain even more.

www.eggheadkids.com - More toys for the little Einstein.

www.drtoy.com - Tips, resources, articles, and the 100 Best Toys list.

www.littlewonderland.com - Exquisite wooden toys.

www.hamleys.com - Classics like the flipping puppy and the dizzy runaround hamster.

www.madallie.com - Toys for happy travelers.

www.sillyasstoys.com - From Airzooka to ant farms.

www.backtobasicstoys.com - Retro toys.

www.playthingspast.com - More vintage toys.

www.world-of-toys.com - For the old-fashioned Etch-A-Sketch we all love.

www.blueorangegames.com - Wooden games sure to become keepsakes.

www.wildplanet.com - Spy toys and Aquapets.

www.jbsnotjusttoys.com - Not just a toy... an experience!

Baby Gifts

www.miracleblanket.com - A swaddler that's worth every penny.

www.bumboseat.com - A revolutionary new concept in infant seats.

www.illustratemyname.com - Personalized gifts.

www.mymiraclebaby.com - Brand name stuff for less.

www.lillamonsters.com - Handmade satin, flannel, and minkee baby blankies.

www.thebaptismblankie.com - In commemoration of baptism.

www.soul-flower.com - Funky baby clothes.

www.polkadotpatch.com - Dressing the spirit of childhood.

www.babyheirlooms.com - Lots of fine keepsakes.

www.lilypadBaby.com - Fashionable and functional gifts.

www.thestylishchild.com - Upscale stuff.

www.firstgift.com - A wide selection of gifts, wrapped for free.

www.thewelcomedguest.com - Gifts to welcome your New One.

www.LandofNod.com - Fab products.

www.greenlittlebeans.com - Handmade stuffed toys.

www.petitbaby.com - Unique European gifts.

www.lucyann.com - Charms.

Fashion for Kids

www.babyrockstar.com - Rock and roll attitude in small packages.

www.converse.com - Design the kid a pair of custom Converse sneakers.

www.friartux.com - Dress-up clothes.

www.nanasboutique.com - Cute stuff.

www.sandboxcouture.com - So the kid can play hard and look good.

www.rainydaywear.com - Fun raingear.

www.magickidsusa.com - For the magic of saving money on quality clothing for kids.

www.LittlebigBoys.com - No purple Barney dinosaurs to be found here.

www.foosies.com - Soft-soled shoes for babies and toddlers.

www.bunnycreek.com - Holiday outfits for boys and girls.

www.oneofakindkid.com - For your unique grandkid.

www.rocknsprouts.com - Edgy, hip threads for the cool little hipster.

www.daddyokidsclothes.com - Classic clothes for the small preppy one.

www.fleecefarm.com - Cozy sweatshirts with trucks, trains, planes, cars .

www.gigglesncurls.com - Girly-girl styles from Europe.

www.underthenile.com - Egyptian cotton clothes that are 100% organic.

www.chicos.com-Chicks of all ages love Chico's clothes .

Fashion, Fitness, and Beauty for Grandmothers

www.hotilids.com - For the official hats of The Hip Grandmas Club.

www.chicos.com - Chicks of all ages love Chico's clothes.

www.stilacosmetics.com - Great makeup.

www.britesmile.com - Brighten your Granny grin.

www.orageski.com - Stylin' ski clothes for snowy trips with the kids.

www.whitehouseblackmarket.com - Black and white fashion.

www.newport-news.com - Hot fashions at cool prices.

www.thatperfectlittleblackdress.com -Vintage little black dresses for all occasions.

www.gypsymoon.com - Fashion for the Stevie Nicks-like grandma.

www.apollolight.com - Light therapy for SADD grandmas.

www.fullspectrumsolutions.com - More light to make life better.

Hip and Healthy Home

www.guardiantechnologies.com - Air sanitizer products.

www.perpetualkid.com - The coolest Band-Aids ever.

www.thetiltedsoupbowl.com - Non-mess soup bowl for sick kids.

www.keepkidshealthy.com - To find the number of your local Poison Control Center.

www.purebrush.com - Kill the germs on your toothbrush.

www.touchlesstrashcan.com - Don't touch that trashcan lid!

www.sharperimage.com - Air purifiers.

www.epipen.com - Every grandmother should learn about Epipens for allergic reactions.

www.stopgerms.org - Tips for a healthy home.

www.thecleanbedroom.com - Organic and natural products, bedding, and mattresses.

www.lowimpactliving.com - Create a green home and save energy and money.

www.healthyhome.com - Non-toxic products made by the people who created the Operating Room filter.

www.apollolight.com-Light therapy for SADD grandmas.

www.thetiltedsoupbowl.com-Non-mess soup bowl for sick kids.

www.EpiPen.com-Every grandmother should learn about EpiPens or allergic reactions.

Activism for Grandmothers

www.raginggrannies.com - Activist-grandmother action league.

www.custodycenter.com - All states now have grandparents' rights laws; check out this site for info.

www.keepachildalive.org - A response to the AIDS epidemic in Africa.

www.grannypeacebrigade.org - Grandmothers for peace.

www.besodoso.com - Clothing for peacemakers.

www.forgottenchildren.net - Proceeds from sales help to abolish child slavery.

www.gawba.org - Grandmothers committed to ending the war in Iraq.

www.towardfreedom.com - A progressive perspective on world events since 1952.

www.grandmothersforpeace.org - Grandmas out to change the world.

www.poetsagainstthewar.org - Poets for peace.

www.madd.org - Mothers aren't the only ones against drunk driving.

www.whirlingrainbow.com - The Grandmother Drum project.

www.ob.org - Operation Blessing: Breaking the cycle of suffering across the world.

www.1000grandmothers.net - Grandmothers fighting for what they believe.

Sleepovers

www.cuddledown.com - For the softest flannel sheets.

www.toocooltshirtquilts.com - Quilts made from your sentimental old T-shirts.

www.econatural.com - 100% bamboo bath towels.

www.babyhammocks.com - Comfy infant sleeping from Australia.

www.bazoongi.com - Sleeping bags for kids.

www.timeoutspots.com - Because even grandmothers need Time Out.

www.barefootdreams.com - Cozy chic robes and throws.

www.crazyforbargains.com - Inexpensive pajamas for grandmothers and kids.

www.gracobaby.com - Every grandmother needs a Graco Pack and Play.

www.barefootdreams.com - Cozy, chic robes and throws.

www.timeoutspots.com - Because even grandmothers need a time out sometimes.

Cooking with Kids

www.craftycookingkits.com - Food that's fun; art that's edible.

www.childrensrecipes.com - Great recipes.

www.spatulatta.com - Free step-by-step videos teach kids about cooking.

www.allheartchefs.com - Chef hats and aprons for the tiny chefs.

www.prairieorchid.com - Oven mitts, baking supplies, and recipes.

www.childrenscookingconnection.com - Provides classes and hands-on cooking parties.

Sites for Teenage Grandkids

www.travelforteens.com - Summer of a lifetime trips for kids.

www.sailcaribbean.com - Summer adventure camps since 1979.

www.cobyusa.com - TVs and DVD players.

www.computercamps.com - Video game design summer camps.

www.thebeanbagchairoutlet.com - Bean bag furniture.

www.gtlorocks.com - A Led Zeppelin tribute band sure to knock the socks off you and the grandteen.

www.creative.com - Electronic music gadgets.

www.toscanaamericana.com - Workshops in Tuscany.

www.sunsetsuzy.com - Surf camp.

www.nyfa.com - Acting and film schools.

www.themachinelive.com - Pink Floyd experience.

www.daisyrock.com - Girl guitars.

www.travelforteens.com - Summer-of-a-lifetime trips for kids.

Potty Training

www.corolle.com - Potty training dolls Emma and Paul.

www.thepottystool.com - A stepping stool so kids can reach the big-people toilet.

www.pottytrainingsolutions.com - Potty training since 1998.

www.pottysong.com - A really annoying customized potty training song that might just do the trick.

www.visionaireproducts.com - Go here to get Peter Potty: the world's only flushable toddler urinal.

www.snipsnsnails.com - Skivvydoodles underwear for boys.

www.justtoiletpaper.com - Funky toilet paper to spark potty interest.

www.pottysong.com - A really annoying, customized potty training song that might just do the trick.

Safety

www.familywatchdog.us - Type in your zip code to find out if predators live in your neighborhood.

www.totfinder.com - Stickers for windows.

www.kidpower.org - Tips, workshops, resources to keep kids safe from strangers.

www.safeview.com - Prevent back-up accidents with a window lens for vans and SUVs.

www.loveourchildrenusa.org - Internet safety for kids.

www.sparky.org - Teach kids about fire safety .

www.babyproofingplus.com - Everything you need to childproof your home.

www.kidco.com - Safety gates.

www.lifefence.com - Child proof your pool.

www.keep-safelockbox.com - Lock up any guns, poisons, medicines.

www.abcsofselfdefense.com - Self defense for kids.

www.yourpersonaldefense.com - Pepper spray disguised as lipstick to protect the grandmother and her brood.

www.GoodDeals.com - Roadside emergency car kits.

www.drugfree.org - Teach your grandkids to Just Say No to drugs.

www.kidpower.org - Tips, workshops, and resources to keep kids safe from strangers.

www.keep-safelockbox.com - Lock up any guns, poisons, or medicines.

www.abcsofselfdefense.com - Self-defense for kids.

Travel

www.combi-intl.com - Car seats and strollers.

www.skjp.com - Kid stuff for on-the-go families.

www.luggagepros.com - Pack your stuff in style.

www.sherrynetherland.com - New York City luxury hotel.

www.congresshall.com - Providing Cape May hospitality since 1816.

www.christopherplace.com - A secluded B&B in the Smoky Mountains of Tennessee.

www.redcaboosemotel.com - Sleep in a train car in Lancaster County, Pennsylvania.

www.smuggs.com - Family ski resort in Vermont.

www.protravelgear.com - Everything you need to travel.

www.albatrosshotel-net - Family-friendly inn in Ocean Grove, New Jersey.

About the Author

Linda Oatman High is the author of more than 20 books for children and teens, as well as a journalist, songwriter, and teacher of writing workshops. Linda is also the grandmother of two boys, Jack and Connor. She babysits Connor two to three days a week, and she loves having an excuse to once again go down sliding boards, hang on monkey bars, and go to Chuck E. Cheese. She is the founder and president of The Hip Grandmas Club (**www.hipgrandma.com**). Info on the author and her work may be found on **www.lindaoatmanhigh.com**.

About The Hip Grandmas Club

The Hip Grandmas Club (online at www.hipgrandma.com) is a community of cool grandmothers who are dedicated to being the best grandmothers we can be while also staying true to ourselves. In person or online, Hip Grandmas Club members share the latest on the best stuff to get (for the grandmas or the grandkids), experiences, advice, laughs, and even Hip Grandma trips and excursions; all while adhering to the Hip Grandma Manifesto.

The top three points of our HGC manifesto:

- Our #1 goal is to remain cool, no matter how old we get or how many grandkids we accumulate. We will be the Queens Of Cool, ruling as ultra-hip matriarchs of our families.

- We will regularly join together for support, bonding, friendship, advice, laughter, fun, and really good chocolate.

- We vow to never, ever wear stereotypical, ugly grandma clothes, drive grandma cars, or have old-lady haircuts. Our goal is to keep up with current trends, technology, music, fashion, and media.

Groove on your grandmother gig and join us at **www.hipgrandma.com**, a community Web site for hip grandmas. Find out about the latest product and trip recommendations, leave a message on the message board, email other hip grandmas, offer your own recommendations, and more.

Welcome to the Hip Grandma's Club. Rock on.